Praise for *Waiting for Your Cat to Bark?*

"In 1999, the Wachowski brothers revolutionized moviemaking with stunning new angles and special effects revealed in *The Matrix*. Now the 'Eisenbrothers' have done the same for business in *Waiting for Your Cat to Bark?* Stunning new angles! Techniques that will be copied for decades. *Cat* is sure to be remembered as the genesis of an important new direction in marketing."

—Roy H. Williams, *New York Times* Best-Selling Author,
The Wizard of Ads Trilogy

"The Web is a democratizing force as the world's largest global brain. It educates everyone on the pros and cons of every product, service, and even person. An educated person doesn't react well to the traditional 'art of manipulation' that most marketers attempt to employ in their campaigns. As a matter of fact, it makes them angry and defensive—like a cat backed into a corner. No one understands this new world of marketing better than the Eisenbergs. *Waiting for Your Cat to Bark?* is the marketing manifesto of our generation. Read it, weep, and then go do something about it."

—Brett Hurt, Founder and CEO of Bazaarvoice,
Founder of Coremetrics, and Shop.org Board Director

"It is easy to buy traffic but persuading that traffic to buy, subscribe, or otherwise take a profitable action is essential. Persuasion Architecture™ provides a framework for companies to better understand and reach customers with more relevant messages that increase the probability of acquiring and serving customers. Traffic cost inflation is a real problem, and this book not only tells you how to allow customers to buy the way they want to buy but makes the entire process accountable. I'll be encouraging the companies I invest in to read it."

—Tod Francis, Managing Partner, Shasta Ventures

"Who's buying? How are they buying? And why do they buy from you? Consumers have been turning away from old media channels and even most methods of advertising to embrace new media. The Eisenbergs have developed a proven methodology for selling in this new environment where the old marketing rules no longer apply. This book will change how you think about marketing. It may even change how you think."

—Rebecca Lieb, Executive Editor, The ClickZ Network

"This book lays out a powerful and fresh way of thinking about personas, persuasion, and marketing in today's increasingly fragmented media environment. If you want a practical guidebook for successfully marketing to today's consumer, then this is a must-read."

—Mark Kingdon, CEO, Organic, Inc.

"*Waiting for Your Cat to Bark?* systematically covers every aspect of critical thinking about customers and prospects a marketer could need in today's complex business world. This is a book you'll reach for every time you begin your strategic planning."

—Susan Bratton, CEO, Cendara, Inc., and Executive Chair
ad:tech Conferences

"With *Waiting for Your Cat to Bark?*, the Eisenbergs have shown us the power of persuasion for marketing. They back up their positions with compelling case studies and great firsthand experience that is priceless. This is a must-read for all marketing professionals and is on my desk."

—Rand Schulman, Chief Active Marketing Officer, WebSideStory

"The Brothers Eisenberg usher us out of the 20th-century age of media and into the 21st-century age of optimization. They show us step-by-step how to leave behind the diminished returns and false expectations of quantity, and how to replace them instead with the more universal appeal and profitability of quality."

—Jeff Einstein, Media Pioneer and Social Critic

"The Eisenberg brothers have done it again! Hot on the heels of their best-selling *Call to Action, Waiting for Your Cat to Bark?* is a guide to the use of personas and Persuasion Architecture™ that will force readers to reconsider all of their marketing efforts. Chock full of "big picture" thinking and great strategic advice, the chapters "Choosing Personas" and "Bringing Personas to Life" are must-reads for anyone serious about marketing. Jeffrey and Bryan force us to rehumanize our audience in a way that drives measurement and forces accountability."

—Eric Peterson, Author, *Web Analytics Demystified* and *Web Site Measurement Hacks*

"*Waiting for Your Cat to Bark?* is a tremendous read. It has fresh ideas and practical solutions for persuading customers to act. I highly recommend this book."

—Ivan R. Misner, Ph.D., *New York Times* Best-Selling Author and Founder of BNI

Waiting for Your Cat to Bark?

Persuading
Customers When
They Ignore
Marketing

BRYAN EISENBERG
JEFFREY EISENBERG
with Lisa T. Davis

NELSON BUSINESS
A Division of Thomas Nelson Publishers
Since 1798

www.thomasnelson.com

Published in Nashville, Tennessee, by Thomas Nelson, Inc.

Nelson Books titles may be purchased in bulk for educational, business, fund-raising, or sales promotional use. For information, please e-mail SpecialMarkets@ThomasNelson.com.

Persuasion Architecture, Persuasion Architect, Persuasion Architecture MAPSuite, and Complexogram are trademarks of Future Now, Inc. and Persuasion Architecture, Inc.

*Offer is only valid for advertisers opening a new U.S. Sponsored Search account through this promotion. Each account requires a non-refundable $5 initial deposit. Advertisers signing up for the Assisted Set-Up service will receive $50 off the service charge. For Self Serve sign ups, a non-refundable $50 credit will be deposited into the account and will be applied towards click charges. Limit one offer per customer, and one use per customer on a single account. Offer may not be combined with any other offers or discounts, separated, redeemed for cash, or transferred. There is a minimum bid requirement of $0.10 per click through. Sellers of certain legally restricted products may require certification at extra cost. Search listings subject to editorial review. Other terms and conditions may apply. See the Advertiser Terms and Conditions when you sign up.

Library of Congress Cataloging-in-Publication Data

Eisenberg, Bryan.
  Waiting for your cat to bark? : persuading customers when they ignore marketing / Bryan Eisenberg and Jeffrey Eisenberg with Lisa T. Davis.
    p. cm.
  ISBN 0-7852-1897-1 (hardcover)
  1. Consumer behavior. 2. On-demand marketing. 3. On-demand advertising. I. Title: Persuading customers when they ignore marketing. II. Eisenberg, Jeffrey. III. Davis, Lisa T. IV. Title.
  HF5415.32.E37 2006
  658.8—dc22   2006005188

Printed in the United States of America
06 07 08 09 QW 5 4 3 2 1

We dedicate this book to the memory of our father,
Santiago Eisenberg
1936–2005

He lived with wisdom, strength,
wealth and honor.
—Pirkei Avot 4:1.

ACKNOWLEDGMENTS

t was the worst of times, and so the best of times passed unacknowledged. In the blink of an eye since I drafted the acknowledgments for *Call to Action* and this moment, Bryan and I have had so much to be grateful for and so many people to thank that we may never get the chance to make it up. With the passing of our father, uncle, and grandmother, we never had the chance or the urge to celebrate our huge success with *Call to Action*.

In the foreword to *Call to Action*, I mused it wasn't exactly the book we intended to write. *Waiting for Your Cat to Bark?* is. Instead of being a book about what we've thought and where we've been, it's a book about what we're thinking and where we're going.

So many people helped make this book happen that naming them all is impossible. Nevertheless, there are those people whose contribution was so great that it would be a sin to leave them unacknowledged.

We thank our friends, Roy and Pennie Williams, for believing in us when there was no good reason to.

We thank our friend, John Quarto-vonTivadar, who helped turn our philosophies and concepts into process and invented Persuasion Architecture™ with us.

We thank our friend, Michael Drew, for his tenaciousness. Without him we would never have become best-selling authors.

We thank our friends, Holly Buchanan and Anthony Garcia, our first best editors, who made this a much better book.

We thank the good people of Thomas Nelson Publishing who believed this was the book that needed to be written.

We thank our friend, Dr. Richard Grant, for his enthusiasm and intellectual rigor.

We thank our friend, Jim Novo, for helping us to refine so many ideas.

We thank our friend, Sam Decker, for reminding us what the reader really cares about.

We thank our friend, David Freeman, for his inspired generosity and insight.

We have been privileged to work with a number of people, expansive of spirit and curious of mind, who were eager to offer their marketing efforts as testing grounds for our ideas. In turn, we have learned much from them. In particular, we'd like to thank our staff, our readers, colleagues, clients, and many others who offered us advice and moral support.

And then there are our families. We lovingly thank our mother, Esther, who bravely supports and encourages us even in the worst of times.

Bryan has Stacey and I have Cindy who love us and put up with us. How can we be more blessed than that? It is possible—Hannah and Sammy are blessings beyond words. We love them dearly.

Without Lisa Davis, one of those family members you get to choose, none of our books would have been written. Her love, loyalty, and hard work are eclipsed only by her talent for extracting what Bryan and I have trapped in our heads. I know Lisa would want to thank Zachary, her brilliant and warm son, for all his patience while this book consumed time that rightfully belonged to him.

And finally, dear reader, we humbly thank you for sharing your all-too-precious time with us. Our greatest wish is that you find in this book something you can use and that you will share it with someone.

Jeffrey Eisenberg
New York City
February 16, 2006

CONTENTS

L ook around. It seems you can't pick up a newspaper or business magazine today without seeing headlines such as:

- ■ "Is Advertising Dead?"
- ■ "The Death of Mass Media"
- ■ "GM Turns Cool to Mass Marketing Advertising"
- ■ "P&G Launches Major Change in Media Spending"

Not since the emergence of television fifty years ago have we seen such a metamorphosis in consumer behavior.

We are witnessing a change in the way media is consumed and the way the entire consumer shopping experience has changed. What's driving this? To paraphrase the former Clinton administration, "It's the Internet, stupid!"

We learned from the dot-com implosion in 2001 that the Internet is neither the "Holy Grail" nor a panacea for marketers. Television, radio, newspapers, and other media are far from being dead. Each remains an important tool in the advertiser's toolkit. Yet, as Bryan and Jeffrey Eisenberg explain in this book, the Internet is the glue that binds customers' experiences in our emerging experience economy.

For marketers, the challenges—and the opportunities—are huge. Advertisers know the old model is broken, and that the old rules do not apply. As broadband has proliferated, the promise of interactivity and creativity on the Web has come to fruition. Consumers are finally in control, and they have become the programmers, consuming media when they want, where they want, and how they want. Video-on-demand, Podcast, TiVo, Yahoo!Go, Google Video, blogs, and more.

We also have a generation of young adults who are now in their twenties and early thirties, who have grown up with interactive technology and are not set in their media-usage habits. With the advent of popular sites like MySpace, Flickr, Facebook, and sixdegrees.com, this group is redefining the roles of traditional media and demand media on *its* terms.

Search marketing is becoming an extremely powerful new way to engage customers, and it makes the Web experience more important than ever. Pay-per-click, a model that did not exist at the end of the last decade, is the fastest growing segment of all advertising.

Clearly we are moving through a time of irrevocable change that has profound implications for businesses large and small. A.G. Lafley, Chairman and CEO of Procter & Gamble, recently said, "We need to reinvent the way we market to consumers. We need a new model. It does not exist."

Until now.

In *Waiting for Your Cat to Bark?* Bryan and Jeffrey Eisenberg dig deeply into the marketing changes we are seeing. They integrate a variety of perspectives and tie together lots of dangling threads, all of which marketers are now called upon to weave into their efforts.

The Eisenbergs speak to the concerns of all marketers who want to navigate intelligently through this emerging media landscape and make a difference on behalf of their companies, within and across channels. They identify why we need to rethink the interconnectedness of marketing and sales, and they offer a smart—and simple—model for looking at customer behavior. Persuasion Architecture is a great framework for becoming an effective marketer in this new world.

Given the changes we are seeing, marketing professionals as well as students of marketing are clearly in need of a playbook to thrive in this new environment. *Waiting for Your Cat to Bark?* is that playbook.

This is an important book. I thoroughly enjoyed it. I am sure you will as well.

Murray Gaylord
Vice President, Brand Marketing
Yahoo! Inc.
January 23, 2006

Waiting for Your Cat to Bark?

This question is really our way of asking, "Are you waiting for your customers to respond the way they used to?"

Many marketers are, and that's a problem.

Cats don't bark—and consumers today don't "salivate on command" like they seemed to a couple of decades ago. Consumers today behave more like cats than Pavlov's pooch. Times have changed—and so must we.

Nobody could have foreseen the challenges today's marketers would face. Twenty years ago, getting through to "over-messaged" customers was like filling a thimble with a fire hose. Imagine what we would have thought then of the multi-tasking, instant-messaging, e-mailing, cell phoning, emoticoning ;-), always on, Web-searching, blogging, TiVo-watching, eBaying customers we now need to reach.

Then, we would have been horrified. Today we're scrambling just to get the job done.

Acquire new customers, deepen relationships with existing customers, reach decision-makers, measure marketing results, generate more leads,

improve lead quality, reconcile selling channels, increase product awareness, close more business, develop the brand—these are our goals as marketers. We understand this language. But the equation has become so
complex that we often lack a framework to describe how one marketing
solution affects the others.

Technology has changed; emerging media are subdividing the masses
into specialized audiences. But the biggest challenge we face is the customer's ability to assert control over the entire process.

While emerging media and technology undermine the effectiveness
of traditional mass-marketing models, they also create unprecedented
opportunity for us to redefine and profit from how we communicate with
customers.

WIIFM: "What's in it for me?"

This book isn't filled with business-school theory. In these pages, we
explain the principles and framework behind the things we do every day.
We give you a framework for modeling interactivity across all your touch
points and for tying all the communications your company creates into a
coherent persuasive system.

In the chapters ahead, we tell a marketing story that has a happy ending. It's not a small story with a simple plot; as marketers, we are not facing a small problem. Through Chapter Thirteen, we lay the groundwork,
examining the interconnected issues in today's marketing landscape. The
balance of the narrative weaves together the elements of our solution.

Along the way, we answer several questions:

- How and why has marketing permanently changed?
  (Chapters One–Six)
- Why do customers respond differently than they used to?
  (Chapters Seven–Thirteen)
- How can you anticipate what customers require? (Chapters
  Fourteen–Twenty-Two)
- How does Persuasion Architecture[1] bridge the new
  marketer/customer gap? (Chapters Twenty-Three–Twenty-Eight)

■ How can you start implementing Persuasion Architecture in your business? (Chapter Twenty-Nine)

We tell this story primarily from a marketing perspective, for marketers and for business owners who are involved in marketing and sales as well as for general students of business and followers of media developments. Our story provides a necessary framework for preparing both marketers and sales staff to manage and respond to the demands emerging media place on them.

Success by multiples!

Waiting for Your Cat to Bark? provides a proven context for rethinking and retooling your customers in a rewired world. We've worked with and helped some of the best and brightest marketers who face the same challenges you face. Persuasion Architecture is enormously practical. It's simple. But it isn't easy. We guarantee, however, that if you start applying these principles to your business, you will get better results—not just by percentages but by multiples.

CHAPTER ONE

Dogs, Cats, and Marketing

I t must have been one of those "light bulb moments." A Russian scientist ambles through his laboratory one day, thoughts of digestive secretions on his mind. Idly he watches a lab-coated assistant lean down to pet one of the dogs.

The dog starts drooling, and this routine sight stops the scientist in his tracks. Assistant pets dog, dog salivates (the involuntary, slobbery confirmation the dog is thinking about food). Yet there is no food in sight. Aha! The assistant always wears his lab coat when he feeds the dog. The dog sees the lab coat and thinks food is on the way.

Most of us, faced with a drooling dog, would simply shake our heads and reach for the nearest paper towel. Not Ivan Petrovich Pavlov, who worked with dogs to help him understand the human digestive system.

To get a handle on the relationship between stimulus and response, Pavlov replaced the lab coat with a sound and began an investigation into the world of conditional reflexes. The rest is history. Pavlov won a Nobel Prize in 1904 for his medical inquiries into the physiology of digestion, but he is best remembered as the man who got dogs to salivate to the sound of a bell.[1]

So what does dog drool have to do with marketing?

Since the time of Pavlov, marketers have been "bell ringers", and customers have played the role of the drooling dog. Bells ring everywhere—there are even ads in urinals—but today fewer customers are panting and whining for a bite. Even worse for marketers, many customers simply find all that bell ringing annoying.

What changed? The bell? The dogs? Why aren't customers responding? And what can marketers do about that?

Cooking up a conditioned response

A conditioned response is a simple form of branding, and you can't create a conditioned response in the blink of an eye. That's why marketers insist on creating the most salient ads possible, then broadcasting those to as many people as possible as frequently as possible.

Here is the recipe for "Customers a la Pavlov":

1. Find your dog and keep him a bit hungry. This takes time.

2. Ring your bell, and offer the dog meat.[2] Dogs love meat; meat is salient. If you try to associate bell ringing with sawdust, the dog will simply ignore you. No self-respecting dog drools for sawdust!

3. Repeat step #2 over and over and over again. When "bell" becomes synonymous with "food" in the canine's gray matter, you can ring the bell, withhold the food, and the dog still salivates.

4. Conditioning can wear off. To keep your dog conditioned, repeat this process frequently.

Modern psychology considers Pavlov's behaviorist experiment an example of "classic conditioning," the goal of which is to instill an association between stimuli (usually external ones like the bell) so that encountering one will bring the other to mind.[3]

Far-reaching implications

In 1909, the implications of Pavlov's results came to the attention of American behaviorist John Broadus Watson, then on the faculty at Johns Hopkins University. In 1930, Watson wrote:

> Give me a dozen healthy infants, well-formed, and my own speci-fied world to bring them up in, and I'll guarantee to take any one at random and train him to become any type of specialist I might select—doctor, lawyer, artist, merchant-chief and, yes, even beggar-man and thief, regardless of his talents, penchants, tendencies, abilities, vocations, and race of his ancestors. I am going beyond my facts, and I admit it, but so have the advocates of the contrary, and they have been doing it for many thousands of years.[4]

Watson gained notoriety through his "Little Albert" experiments, in which he conditioned a fear response in an eleven-month-old boy, using a white rat and a loud sound.[5] Forced to leave academia when he was caught in a sex scandal involving the student who assisted him in this research, Watson turned his attention to advertising and went to work for J. Walter Thompson (now JWT):

> . . . where, using techniques from his behavioral psychology, he showed that people's preferences between rival products were not based on their sensory qualities but on their associations. He went on to develop the selling of products like Maxwell House Coffee, Pond's Cold Cream, Johnson's Baby Powder and Odorono (one of the first deodorants). By 1924 he was one of the four vice-presidents of this very successful agency.[6]

"So here we have J.B. Watson," wrote Chris Locke in *Chief Blogging Officer*, "father of American behaviorism, packing up all he knows about eliciting the Pavlovian slobber reaction, and wholesaling it to Madison Avenue."[7]

Through men like Pavlov and Watson, the seeds for over half a century's worth of marketing practice were planted, then nourished by the "science" of behaviorism and its successful application in the spheres of marketing.

"Tom" foolery

Pavlov used dogs because their digestive systems are similar to those of humans. As all his equipment was set up to accommodate dogs, Pavlov carried out his conditional reflex experiments on dogs.[8]

We suspect Pavlov would have had a harder time—and wonder what it might have meant to the development of behaviorist marketing practice—had he been working with cats. You can classically condition a response in many creatures, but the ease depends in large part on the nature of your subject and the reinforcement you use.

One basic difference between cats and dogs is motivation.[9] Centuries of cat and dog humor captures the stereotypes: A dog wants to please you; a cat couldn't care less. Dogs are devoted and loving and selfless. Cats are aloof, indifferent, and self-indulgent. Dogs are social and act in ways that maintain and support the social order. Cats are solitary and act in ways that benefit themselves.

Cat Haiku

The food in my bowl
Is old, and more to the point
Contains no tuna.

Most problems can be
Ignored. The more difficult
Ones can be slept through.

Am I in your way?
You seem to have it backwards:
This pillow's taken.[10]

Yes, a cat may come running when she hears you going for the can opener, and with enough effort you can teach her to roll over on command some percentage of the time. Ultimately, though, her engagement with you lasts only as long as she wants it to last. A cat is not out to please you; she's in it for herself.

She is not, and never will be, a dog.

Consumer branding: calling all cats

Early marketers, supported by Pavlov's research and studies with human subjects, attempted to "prove" that when businesses rang the right bell the right number of times, they could command desire and behavior in their audience through branding alone. Early successes helped them feel advertising gave them control over their audiences.

When the available advertising media choices were limited and communities were more localized, people's exposure to alternative experiences was restricted. It seemed possible that this theoretical control, or behavior-centeredness, of marketing was the key. Customers did, indeed, appear to salivate to marketing's bells and responded by buying the most heavily marketed goods and services.

Few anticipated the full effect of blossoming media options on the behaviorist marketing models. Even as late as the mid-1980s, people looked upon burgeoning media—broadcast and cable television and radio—as growing vehicles for delivering messages to even larger audiences who were predisposed to "devour information and constantly clamor for more."[11] Expanding media markets seemed to offer brilliant opportunities to ring better bells for increasingly more dogs.

Even a casual reading of a newspaper's business section, with headlines that herald the death of mass-marketing and advertising, reveals the opportunities haven't played out the way we'd hoped.

To everyone's disappointment, emerging media are shattering behaviorist marketing tenets. Businesses are not in control of the strings; they can command neither desire nor response. Customers now have access to an unprecedented amount of information and can communicate any time and place they please. As media fragments, so does the "mass" in mass-marketing.

The window that emerging media has opened for us reveals a personal-experience economy, in which customers are in control. Brand is defined in customers' minds by their personal experiences with a particular product or service. Attentive only to the information that matters to them, customers are behaving a lot more like cats than like Pavlov's dogs.

Interactivity has changed the nature of marketing. Marketers must now reach beyond their traditional roles of raising awareness and driving traffic and extend themselves into the more intimate world of sales and customer relations. They are now responsible for creating powerful "persuasive systems" that anticipate and model customer needs, personalize information and processes to meet those needs, and then measure the return on investment for every discrete process in that system.

Technology may evolve at a pace that leaves us breathless, but the essential qualities of human behavior aren't nearly that transitory. The road may have changed, but those traveling on the road haven't.

We are not, and have never been, the metaphoric equivalent of Pavlov's dogs.

Actually, when it comes to consumer behavior, we've always been like cats. All it took was a little media fragmentation and a critical mass of information for management to notice. Understanding the "What's in it for me?" focus in our customers' behavior patterns is central to success.

We don't suggest you find better ways to ring better bells. Instead, we present you with the context for celebrating meows.

CHAPTER TWO

Experiencing the Brand

Mass marketing may be going the way of the dinosaur, but we would never suggest the principle of branding is on its deathbed. The need to establish and sustain name recognition and associative benefits will always be a part of the competent marketer's stock in trade. However, the complex and interconnected relationships between emerging media and the information they now make available mean that name recognition and associations alone are insufficient. Increasingly, customers are associating brand not with a message but with their entire experiences surrounding the product or service.

In other words, branding is now more about what you do than what you say.

Because people have complex motivations, marketers have worked to establish meaningful connections between their products or services and the customers' felt needs. Very often, these branding efforts have drawn on Maslow's hierarchy of needs.

Abraham Maslow and his hierarchy

All of us prioritize our needs in a predictable manner, starting with "deficit" needs—those most basic to survival.

In 1943, psychologist Abraham Maslow represented these ascending levels of human needs in the form of a pyramid, with deficit needs represented at its base. Higher levels represented more complicated "being" (or growth) needs. As a person adequately meets the needs of one level, she is able to move progressively higher on the pyramid, to meet the needs of the next level.

For example, in the wake of a catastrophe, as otherwise law-abiding citizens often discover, the search for food and other basic necessities overrides every other consideration. There's little time for the luxury of esteem needs when your survival is at stake. Once you're full, hunger ceases to be such a powerful motivator . . . for most of us anyway. Once food needs have been satisfied, they cease to motivate behavior. You start thinking about other things.

Maslow identified self-actualization—the desire to become everything you are capable of becoming—as the overarching human need.[1] This is not a deficit need; it's a growth need, and fulfilling it is generally a lifelong process. Maslow acknowledged that even when our deficit needs are met, the need to be true to our own definition of ourselves influences our attempts to satisfy *every* category of need on the pyramid.

Marketing and advertising folks have used Abraham Maslow's hierarchy of needs as a formula for motivating customers to buy: Target the appropriate need, and you can create the compelling associative cues that elicit desire. It's not fool-proof, of course. Target a level too low, and you risk creating messages that customers ignore (their need is already satisfied). Target too high on the pyramid, and customers may not be ready to hear you (they're still focused on meeting a more basic need).

An inventory of modern western civilization suggests that deficit needs, for the majority of us, are readily satisfied. But very few people achieve complete self-actualization in their lifetimes. Thus, marketers have grown increasingly fond of targeting the top of the Maslow's hierarchy, imbuing their products or services with an ability to help customers "be the best they can be." And to a great degree, this accounts for much of the over-reaching that often damages more than it benefits a brand.

Problems and solutions

If you understand the customer's need—if you can explain how your particular brand scratches their particular type of itch—then branding remains a perfectly viable option. We would never deny the effectiveness of creating desire through a broadcast model that builds associative cues between a product or service and a felt need. However, identifying needs and positioning solutions in the marketplace isn't as straightforward as it used to be.

Twentieth-century marketing history has been about introducing categories of products and solutions that previously didn't exist. As the playing field was populated with an increasing number of competitors whose products or services solved the same problem, discrete marketing categories evolved.

Let's look at what happened to fizzy drinks. Soda fountains were patented in 1819, and the first bottled soda water was available in 1835. The Irish developed ginger ale in 1851. In the 1860s, someone coined the term "pop" for the limited but popular array of carbonated beverages.

That Texas staple, Dr Pepper, was invented in 1885. Coke in 1886. Pepsi in 1898. The American Bottlers of Carbonated Beverages formed in 1919. In 1966, this organization changed its name to the National Soft Drink Association.[2]

From discrete, localized products evolved the soft-drink category. And alongside the explosion of liquid fizz options came the need to tie customer desire not just to the product but also to the category. Marketing's goal was to establish the brand as the soft drink of choice.

When there were fewer competitors in the market, it was easier for each company to anchor their associative cues in the actual need their products satisfied. Early marketing for soft drinks could capitalize on the unique, delicious, refreshing, thirst-quenching qualities of the brand, and it was up to the product to deliver on that promise.

But as the number of competing, equally refreshing soft drinks increased, so did the need to anchor the product to something larger than the actual problem it solved.

To distinguish themselves from the crowd, marketers aimed higher on Maslow's pyramid and devised messages addressing their audience's need for self-actualization. So it was that Coca-Cola taught the world to sing and became the "real thing." Choosing Coke meant being authentic and part of a global experience. Pepsi-Cola became the drink of a New Generation. If you drank Pepsi, you were a socially adept participant in a happy, happening experience.

When problems and solutions are difficult to articulate

In other situations, the need and the solution are not as easy to communicate. This is especially true where the product or service exists in a category that is nearly impossible to differentiate. An excellent example is the personal computer, which has multiple categories of buyers in both individual and business flavors.

IBM was wildly successful in establishing name recognition and building its brand on associative cues that promoted the reliability of the product, the efficiency of the technology behind the product, and the leadership of the company. IBM became synonymous with computer the way Kleenex became synonymous with facial tissue. Every emerging competitor identified themselves as IBM-compatible. The success of the IBM brand made it possible for Microsoft and Intel, with their Windows environment, to dominate the market despite the fact Apple offered a superior product.

The branding problem for computers is that neither businesses nor individuals think about their need for a computer in universal terms. A computer does not satisfy a thirst or hunger or a desire to belong. And no two people need exactly the same computer for precisely the same reasons. People buy computers as a means to an end: for what the computer allows them to do, in the same way that people buy drills because they need holes. However, branding efforts that focused on computing tasks like accounting, gaming, or word processing failed to create a mass brand or to address a core need.

Branding in this context is much more difficult; there is no single association upon which to anchor the brand. To the customer looking to purchase a computer, brand takes a back seat to distribution, price, reliability, and service. And while you can try to brand for these qualities, they certainly don't address the ultimate benefits of purchasing a computer.

Moreover, traditional reviews and consumer-generated media can quickly undermine marketing's frontal view by relating information that conflicts with a company's claims regarding distribution, price, reliability, and service. For example, Jeff Jarvis, playing David to Dell's Goliath, proved this with a single blog post: "Dear Mr. Dell."[3] Jarvis's post about his negative experience resulted in a deluge of negative sentiment that is now part of the information package Dell's marketers have to address.

Taking advantage of audience fragmentation allowed Alienware, a high-end personal computer marketer, to establish itself as a dominant brand in the computer gaming niche. They spoke to those customers who could articulate their need not through the anchoring of associative cues but through the specific packaging of the information they presented about a superior gaming experience.

When it comes to marketing computers, it's difficult to create a mass brand. Alienware and software programs like QuickBooks, which offers an accounting solution for smaller businesses, have been able, however, to create strong brands that are associated with a specific solution for a smaller segment of the population. They have done this by focusing on how they package the information and shape the experience around the brand.

A new playing field for bell-ringing

In crafting their messages, many traditional marketers went well beyond the basics of Pavlovian conditioning and the obvious natural associations between the problem and the solution, between the need and a customer's motivation to satisfy that need. Did this work? Well, no one could dispute the fact that Coke and Pepsi are dominant players in the soft-drink category.

Will it continue to work? Mary Minnick, president of Coke's global marketing, innovation, and strategy, recognizes the challenge of selling both Coke the product and Coke the brand. "In order to do this, 'traditional media is not enough,' she said. TV advertising has grown from 800 to 8,000 ads daily, and the increasing clutter makes the medium a less effective tool to advertise the company's core brands . . ."[4]

Success depends on the ability of businesses to adapt to a rapidly changing market characterized by an exponential growth of products and services clamoring for our attention. At the same time, there has been an exponential increase in the number of media options available to customers, as well as an increase in the amount of time those customers are engaging with media.

Media have always been the coveted venues for anchoring associative cues and building name recognition. And people are spending more and more time with media. A Ball State University study reported that the average person spends 11.7 hours a day with media. Even the "least media-active person" spends 5.25 hours with media.[5] According to Jeff Einstein, media pioneer and social critic, "Media addiction is not only our primary addiction in the twenty-first century, but it is also the primary enabler of all other addictions, both licit and illicit."[6]

This should be joyful news for broadcast branding, but as we will discuss in the next chapter, the proliferation of media is a double-edged sword for marketers. All those media options alter the nature and quantity of available information. They expand the resources customers can turn to. They subdivide the "masses" into increasingly narrower, self-identified audiences.

It doesn't help that the generations who have grown up with these media options are becoming more cynical and more demanding. These days, people's BS meters operate in high alert mode—people can spot a false claim, a hyped pitch, or an over-reaching associative clue in a nanosecond.[7] And they can discount and ignore it in the next nanosecond. They know that using a product isn't what makes them special. Calls for transparency, less hype, and the ability to see businesses as real—values that characterized the 1960s and 70s—now combine with an unprecedented opportunity for people to define themselves more narrowly and accurately.

We have described both ends of the branding continuum, from what is essentially a simple sale (a soft drink) to a complex sale (a computer). In both cases, the conditioned response model—traditional marketing— is no longer working.

If people and their needs were less complicated, the inevitable outcome of traditional marketing would be to limit the dominant players. The big guys simply would swallow the competition. The fact that this is not happening defies the expectations of bell-ringers everywhere.

The powerful influences of emerging media are redefining the parameters of bell-ringing. Customers are not making their choices based on name recognition or associative cues alone although these can influence their decisions. The most important factors for customers today are the experience itself and the information available about that experience.

Lots of choices. Lots of information. It's the most experience-based economy we've ever known, and in this economy, the experience has become the brand.

CHAPTER THREE

Friction and Customer Experience

There's an adage: "The intelligent man learns from his own experience; the wise man learns from the experience of others." These days, the opportunities to be wise are plentiful.

Our consumer experiences are composed of our use of a product or service itself—whether or not it met our expectations—as well as the experience of selecting and purchasing the product or service. Beyond that, and often in place of that, our experience includes what we read about the experiences of others.

Experience is entirely about "value in context." Positive or negative, value is in the eye of the beholder. Whether something tastes like fine champagne or cod-liver oil, the value of the resulting experience will depend on whether the need was for a classy beverage or a relieving purge.

To fully understand the experience economy in which we now operate, it helps to review—briefly and rather simply—the history of commerce, so we can identify the trends still operating today.

From the merchants of the Middle Ages to the e-businesses of today, the goal has been to remove friction from the sales process. Friction results from the customers' experiences of cognitive dissonance, an inability to feel that the sales process alone has met their ultimate needs. The piece missing for customers is confidence—the lower the degree of confidence, the higher the friction. Smart merchants know the secret to success is not to make it easier for the seller, but to make it easier for the buyer.

The introduction of new technologies has always provided lubrication to ease the friction. Transportation technology, communication technology, and payment technology have all improved over the years. Those merchants who took advantage of the new technologies prospered. Those who pooh-poohed them were left behind.

So . . . the history of commerce. How did it all start? What has changed? And what hasn't?

To market, to market

Whether you believe history's first sale involved an apple or the follow-up to a wink, barter was the earliest and most rudimentary means of exchanging value. You have something, I have something else, and so we haggle over relative values and attempt to trade. Barter offers a subjective, intimate, and immediate evaluation of experience.

Commerce became more efficient when larger numbers of people gathered to participate in the exchange. With marketplaces, it became easier to gauge the value of the experience, but the experience itself remained relatively inefficient. While it was possible to trade labor or goods, these things were valuable only if the consumer needed them right then. If I needed chickens, but you had only eggs, it would be hard for us to trade.

Enter the concept of stored value. If we could agree on the standard, then shells, gold, salt, or even beads could represent value. Later, we could exchange this value "placeholder" to get what we wanted. As this method of trade gained universal acceptance, the advantages became clear: it allowed customers to accumulate value and trade it conveniently when the circumstances were right.

Still, even with universal stored values, we can't, to quote Mick Jagger, always get what we want.

Merchant

Out of this rather disorganized, producer-based market economy emerged a more specialized merchant economy that manufactured or sold products or labor. As businesses specialized into niche markets, and as stalls in transient marketplaces gave way to permanent shops, it became even more convenient for people to get *what* they wanted *when* they wanted it.

Notice the trend here: the customer is gaining more control in the process. As customers gain more control, they gain more confidence.

But things were not always forward-moving. Commerce took several steps backward during the Dark Ages. The collapse of the Roman Empire disrupted communications and transportation. A third-century Roman would have been horrified to discover in the economic landscape of the tenth century that it was virtually impossible to get his fine Egyptian cotton tunics!

Oversimplifying our way through the history of the Dark Ages, we see the development of commercial districts—concentrations of shops, first in discrete areas throughout a city, then in the High Street and culminating in our modern-day malls. These economic centers combined a variety of shopping experiences—food and entertainment among them—to draw in customers and encourage trade.

On the road again

Markets and merchant concentrations were geography-dependent. Location was critical. Certainly trades were made across great distances, but these were hardly convenient and rarely cost-effective for the average consumer.

As transportation and communication networks grew, the concept of a catalog evolved. Thus, a merchant like Mr. Sears was able to trade with numerous other merchants, centralize the offerings through a printed medium, and provide products to people in locations that were remote to both Mr. Sears and his wholesalers (sound kind of like the Internet?).

The advent of a reliable postal service and the telephone made it possible for some services to become less geography-dependent. A financial advisor didn't have to work on Main Street for customers to take advantage of his services. Overcoming the limitations of locality by bringing the message and the product or service directly to the customer further reduced the friction points that limited buying behavior.

Beyond the printed page: radio and television

New technology drastically changed the commercial landscape even more. Radio presented an unprecedented opportunity for broadcast marketing as an alternative to catalog merchandizing. Not only could a company like Procter & Gamble transport to remote locations, they could also reach a much larger audience.

Television magnified the effects of radio. As the television became a living room staple, marketers found they were able to buy ads that reached 90 percent of their audience. Customers, reveling in the experience of availability and ease of access, could learn of products or services they otherwise might not have known existed.

Because radio and television are intrusive media, they offer marketers an edge over passive media when it comes to capturing the attention of listeners. Passive (sight-based) media—newspapers, magazines, billboards, direct mail, e-mail—requires the focused attention of the user in order to process the message. Intrusive (sound-based) media, such as radio and television, have the ability to regain the listener and viewer's attention once they have lost focus.

Both serve a purpose. Passive media effectively reach customers who are actively looking for a product or service. Intrusive media, on the other hand, surpass passive media in their ability to get a message lodged into the customer's brain. Even when sound is droning quietly in the background, our minds filter the input. When something aural captures our interest, we pay attention. Small wonder that a television in every living room and a radio in every car thrilled marketers—and that media-buying became a science as well as an art.

With radio, television, and print media as advertising venues, the behavior-centeredness of marketing held sway. Customers appeared to salivate to bell-ringing and responded by buying the most heavily marketed goods and services.

At its height—a time when the last generation of marketers cut their teeth on network and matured with cable—television gave the illusion that these marketing relationships would remain relatively simple. Businesses could imagine they'd solved the communication friction points that impeded sales.

Big mistake. New technologies were about to make it easier for the customer to buy. But those technologies still had not removed all the friction points from the sale. In fact, they introduced a few of their own.

Fall to pieces

At the same time network television was fulfilling the promise of behavioral marketing beyond anyone's wildest dreams, mass media vehicles were beginning to fragment.

In radio, the AM dial became the also-ran as FM channels multiplied, providing numerous alternatives to niche audiences.

In television, the advent of cable fractured the viewing habits of an audience no longer limited to three networks. In North America, cable and satellite television have permeated the landscape, serving up an unbelievable smorgasbord of choice. All of this choice—the result of consumer desire for content that appeals to diverse interests—has contributed enormously to the fragmentation of the broadcast audience. As a result, it has become virtually impossible for businesses to reach 90 percent of their potential market.

Addressing AdTech's 2005 conference, Sean Dee, the Chief Marketing Officer of Hard Rock Cafe, illustrated the effect of fragmentation with this example: In 1985, more than half the people in the country—65 million viewers—tuned in to *The Cosby Show*. Today, a top-rated television show does well to net 20–25 million viewers.

Interactive TV

Television as a specific venue for sales, rather than a mouthpiece for advertising, blossomed with infomercials. Infomercials quickly evolved into interactive television. Companies like HSN and QVC were able to take a product and provide the viewer with a depth of information local merchants and catalogs could rarely match. In a focused environment, sellers could remove products from boxes, show them in realistic settings from all angles, field questions from the "Medialand" audience, and supply rousing testimonials. It was like a catalog experience on steroids, delivered remotely.

More choice, more control

Each phase in our cursory history of commerce has been about the seller providing the buyer with a more delightful experience. It's been about reducing friction in the customer's buying process.

As customers have grown more and more demanding, the seller has had to work overtime to serve up a richer, more customized experience. Those sellers who have come out ahead are those willing to embrace new technology and advertising mediums.

Our history of commerce ends with the interconnectivity of the Internet and all its associated wireless technologies. On the Internet, everyone has the opportunity to see what other people are saying, uncensored, about virtually anything. For the first time, customers can reach far beyond the advice of their neighbors and friends to learn of others' experiences.

It's nothing short of amazing.

Positioned for huge success, the 2003 film, *Gigli*, was star-studded—featuring Ben Affleck and Jennifer Lopez with appearances from Christopher Walken and Al Pacino. Martin Brest *(Beverly Hills Cop* and *Scent of a Woman)* was the director. Expectations ran high. But on the night of the east coast debut, audiences and critics dubbed it a flop. When *Gigli* opened three hours later on the west coast, ticket sales were appallingly low. Communication of the east coast experience was so swift and unequivocal, those across the country didn't even bother to turn out.

Into cyberspace

New technology. Increased communication. Increased fragmentation. Increased customer control. Are you seeing the trend? It can be daunting. New media emerge, and the audience seems to shrink—what's a seller to do?

This is not a gloom-and-doom story. Fortunately, there's plenty of good news too. Fragmentation has allowed smart sellers to create customized, niche-based messages. Selling big by selling small. Micro-marketing rather than mass-marketing. Remember Alienware and QuickBooks?

Just as FM radio and cable eroded the supremacy of the mass market, the Internet's "ability to gather global demand for niche products means those niches can now sell enough in total to be substantial markets." The net's capacity also creates an unprecedented opportunity within the "long-tail" of low-selling products.[1] And the effect is not limited to the occasional product here or there. Amazon CEO Jeffrey Bezos figures 20 percent of Amazon's book sales fall outside the 130,000 titles offered through chain superstores.[2]

This trend of aggregating demand has affected countless businesses that never could have made it in the mass market. In the same way, cable made possible an array of niche channels like the *Food Network*, the *History Channel*, and the *Sci-Fi Channel*. Cable offers the viewer 24-hour news, sports, and movies, but the Internet offers 24-hour everything— limitless programming via limitless numbers of channels. It's the most egalitarian, far-reaching marketplace we've ever known.

With the Internet, commerce has evolved to a point where nobody has a dominant voice. Nobody controls the technology. Virtually anybody can start a business with nothing more than an Internet connection and a way of receiving payment. And with just a few clicks, virtually anyone can publish virtually anything at virtually no cost.

The experience economy

Each step along our commercial timeline solved a problem, reduced customer friction by increasing confidence, and provided a more satisfying experience. Businesses hammered out the details to their customers' delight. In its heyday, Macy's offered a delightful department-store experience. But increased competition raised the bar for the "delight factor."

As competition increases, it's harder to get customers. So the focus must become understanding and delighting the customer. Big box stores like Target, Kmart, and Wal-Mart made searching for specialized items at

Macy's a less delightful experience. Competition has always come in the form of better production and performance, better logistics, better financial opportunities, and better communications. The integration of these factors produces the experience.

In a strange way, we've come almost full circle. With so many options from which to choose, increasingly sophisticated consumers have access to copious amounts of information. And the differentiating factor in the exchange is, once more, "what you get."

Our current market demands information-based packaging. Buyers crave information about the experience, but sellers remain stingy in sharing information. Millions of customers are packaging their experiences and making them available to millions of other customers. Businesses need to do the same, and that frightens many marketers. Yet publishing all the information a customer needs to feel confident presents unlimited opportunities for resolving the friction that prevents buying. (In Chapter Twenty-Four, we explain our technique for removing friction in the buying and selling processes.)

It's all about experience . . . *theirs*

The experience economy, first identified by management thinkers, B. Joseph Pine II and James H. Gilmore, is upon us. It signifies the final blow to the notion of mass marketing. Today, the experience of the product or service—the experience of the exchange itself—defines delight and ultimately spells success or failure for the business and the brand.

Experience is not objective. And it is your *customer's* perception of the experience that you must strive to improve. The more you reduce friction in your sales process, the more you accommodate your customer's buying process, the more confidence the customer gains, the better the customer experience.

The increased intimacy of that experience is what allows customers to ascribe a deeper connection and more value to products and services. The structuring of that intimacy is the goal of Persuasion Architecture.

CHAPTER FOUR

Why Marketing Is Simple But Hard

M arketing success rests firmly on the shoulders of a viable product experience—the product or service must have intrinsic merit. As marketers, it isn't our job to develop, produce, transport, or fund great products (though we may think it should be). Production, logistics, finance, and communication all fit together to reinforce the experience.

When you think about it, all areas of a business ultimately support the job of selling.

In 1917, an article by British businessman George Smith appeared in *System*. With their integrative ideas and customer focus, Smith's words still resonate today:

> The cleverest salesman in the world, the best writer of advertisements in the world, cannot, alone, continue to make sales of anything which has not in itself selling merit; and, on the other hand, the worst salesman in the universe, supplemented by the worst

copy-writer in the universe, cannot avoid making sales of something which has in it the selling idea . . . Real selling begins with the
conception of the article, goes through every branch of the business, and the salesman should be not a mere individual but the
interpreter to the buyer . . . Real selling is mutual; it is bringing to
a man some thing that he needs or wants . . . Selling is not a separate division of business; it is business . . . The selling ideas are put
in by the factory, and therefore the factory should know the consumer . . . The best is that which the public determines to be best.[1]

Sounds easy, doesn't it? But it's actually pretty hard to achieve.

We've explained the premise behind the challenges of the experience
economy we are facing. Our observations aren't new. Lots of people are
looking at the lay of the land and reaching the same conclusion. We all see
what is happening, and we intuitively understand that marketing must
evolve if we want to hang on to our plump bottom lines.

We acknowledge that production, logistics, and finance are intimately
a part of the big picture of business and marketing success.[2] Certainly a
disconnect occurs when the marketing lives apart from the reality of the
product experience. When marketers go out with a budget, and that
budget is meant to communicate the wonderful experience customers will
have, things fall apart if all the other factors aren't lined up to deliver the
promised experience.

For purposes of this book, we'll set aside these factors and concen-
trate on why executing the simplicity of George Smith's ideas is so difficult. In developing our story, we focus on communications—the
interactivity of the media and the packaging of information—as the
important piece marketers can directly influence and shape. We need to
understand the effective role of communications in an emerging-media,
experience economy.

Being reasonable

While we *can* be cynical, we are being neither cynical nor unrealistic.
Obviously we need to strike a balance between delivering exactly what the

customer wants and satisfying the production, logistics, and finance constraints of business.

Imagine a business model that offers a four-course gourmet meal, lovingly prepared to individual dietary specifications, and delivered to the door at the end of a customer's workday—all for a dollar. Who wouldn't sign up? Notwithstanding a customer's desire for such service, clearly, this model wouldn't mesh with anyone's business objectives . . . unless bankruptcy was the objective.

Basically, though, customers are conditioned to be reasonable, and businesses, by and large, are also reasonable. Our philosophy and principles are for those businesses who, within the confines of profitability and integrity, truly want to deliver the experience the customer needs in order to feel delighted. (If you happen to be among the "notable exceptions" who operate on bad faith, then what we have to say in this book will not be relevant to you. In fact, we encourage you to read something else.)

The pressures of inside-the-bottle syndrome

It isn't inherently difficult to articulate or execute George Smith's simplicity. The practice itself isn't hard at all. The problem is our perspectives have a tendency to cloud the picture. And when customers get to cast votes based on *their* unique perspectives, well, you can see where the job can really start to spin into frenzy.

The most obvious perspective we have to cope with is what we call inside-the-bottle syndrome. On a day-to-day basis, we are all wrapped up in the most pressing needs of our jobs or businesses. And the needs most pressing, unless we have direct contact with customers, are the ones right in front of us at that moment. Everyday pressures—producing reports, helping the company realize an upwards-trending graph of net profits, making the perfect pot of coffee, cutting costs, and responding to changes made in other areas of the company—affect the experience we are trying to communicate.

After hours, days, weeks, months, even years of so-called "real-life perspective," it becomes easier and easier to slip into the abyss of the company bottle. You become trapped and have only a blurry vision of what's going on outside. Competitors look morphed and out of proportion. The label on your own company bottle is hard to read.

It's from deep inside this bottle that some of the most bloodletting business decisions are made—giving airline passengers fewer peanuts to snack on or outsourcing telephone customer service to Asia. You can't trace the effects of actions like these back to profit-and-loss statements; they don't have immediate consequences to the bottom line, certainly nothing that can be measured on a monthly or yearly basis. Inside the bottle, all systems are go.

Outside the bottle, a frequent flyer counts a total of three peanuts in her snack bag. Her husband doesn't understand a word the technical support person says in trying to solve a computer problem. The customers' perceptions change; your brand is blemished. And inside the bottle, you and your team are laughing at the water cooler, thinking all is well. All is well.

Incremental business changes can erode relationships. A friendship isn't ruined when someone forgets a birthday, but a progressive series of slights might lead to estrangement. You don't stop shopping at your favorite grocery store because they no longer bag your groceries, but suffer enough cost-cutting compromises, and you may shift your allegiance.

Inside the bottle, we lack a critical perspective. Inside the bottle, we hear the concerns of the business; we think the way the business thinks, from the perspective of the business and the bottom line. We can see people are buying what we have to offer—the very fact we are still in business seems to confirm we are satisfying customers.

After all, satisfying customers is the goal, isn't it? Inside the bottle, all is well.

Frederick F. Reichheld, director of Bain & Company, cautioned businesses against focusing on satisfaction at the expense of developing loyalty: "It's not how satisfied you keep your customers, it's how many satisfied customers you keep."[3] The automobile industry brags about impressive satisfaction rates of 90 percent among their customers. Yet repurchase rates are half that number.

Reichheld writes, "Bain & Company's research has shown that in business after business, 60% to 80% of customers who defect to a competitor said they were satisfied or very satisfied on the survey just prior to their defection." Given that satisfaction is an inherently fleeting experience, the key for businesses lies in "watching what specific customers pay, not just what they say." Loyalty is a far more accurate measure of how a business is performing.[4] Loyalty reflects an outside-the-bottle view.

As Peter Drucker, author and one of the greatest management theorists in the business world would have said, the purpose of business is to make and keep a customer. That hasn't changed; it's only become more important.

Experience is crafted from many different components. The pressures of achieving business objectives can lead to decisions that alienate customers. Determining the causes can be frustrating since it's virtually impossible to identify exactly which straw broke the camel's back. Would our frequent flyer's husband have tried harder to understand the computer-support technician in India if the computer itself were extremely satisfying?

Whenever we hear the big THOOP sound as we chat with our clients, we stop to celebrate. It's the thrilling sound of a company pulling its head out of its bottle.

Traffic or conversion?

Traditionally, one of marketing's tasks is to increase traffic. You want more sales? Just bring in more people. It's a no-brainer, isn't it? So when a business wants to ramp up sales, they turn to marketers to create messages that will bring more customers. Those marketers, in turn, inevitably focus on devising more effective messaging or creating incentives rather than focusing on the quality of a customer's experience.

Unfortunately, advertising campaigns and incentive programs have a life cycle—they do not provide permanent solutions for the underlying problem.

In the early days at Future Now, Inc., we would explain to clients that bringing more people into a system that does a poor job of converting them into buyers is purely a waste of money. The math makes no sense.

Let's say ten thousand new customers come to you each month. Two hundred of them complete their transactions. This means you have a monthly conversion rate of 2 percent. If you double the number of people who come each month, at the same conversion rate you'll have approximately four hundred sales a month.

Yes, you increased sales by increasing traffic. Congratulations.

But suppose you increased your conversion rate a measly two percentage points, to 4 percent? Now, without spending a penny of your marketing budget, those ten thousand customers net you *four hundred* sales a month. By improving the experience, you could achieve what it otherwise would take an additional ten thousand prospects each month to accomplish. *Now* you have a reason to acquire more traffic and reap the full benefits. Fifteen thousand customers at a four percent rate of conversion? That's eight hundred sales a month! In addition, an improved experience is far more likely to delight your customers—and delighted customers become repeat customers.

Any conversion process is like a leaky bucket—you pour water in, and water spurts out all the holes. You can keep adding more and more water to the bucket, or you can patch up the holes. Clearly, patching the holes first makes much better sense. We figure it's like the cart-before-the-horse thing. Create the delightful experience first then drive the traffic.

Accentuate the tangibles?

We operate in a culture that gives more credence to hard, cold facts than fuzzy values that are just as real but, regrettably, are intangible. We can measure the dollar value of a cost reduction. We can correlate that with productivity and all sorts of other business concerns. However, we have no reliable ways for measuring how these compromises affect the customer's benchmark experience and damage the relationship. Nor, as we've mentioned, do we have ways to tie the full impact of a compromise to the bottom line.

We do know the deck often is stacked heavily against those who prioritize the intangibles. For example, Wall Street has a problem with Costco, the warehousing business that is comparable to BJ's Wholesale Club or Wal-Mart's SAM's Club, which offers a similar warehouse experience. Wall Street argues that James Sinegal, CEO of Costco Wholesale, is not only generous to his customers but also to his employees, paying

Costco workers almost half again as much as rivals pay their staff and offering them a compassionate health-care plan.[5] One Wall Street analyst, Bill Dreher of Deutsche Bank, complained that at Costco, "it's better to be an employee or a customer than a shareholder."[6]

Sinegal mandates markups in the teens, compared to retail markups of up to 50 percent. Good wages and benefits for workers means Costco has an extremely low rate of turnover among employees and experiences considerably less employee theft. With minimal advertising, Costco has generated an almost cult-like following of loyal customers, unlike the other deep-discounters. And even the shareholders appear to be happy, as Costco stock performs very nicely, thank you very much. This is in spite of Wall Street's penalization.

Analysts say Sinegal is too generous to his employees and that the company could clearly charge more. Sinegal keeps resisting Wall Street pressure to conform to their profit demands. Where Wall Street sees waste, Sinegal simply sees good business.

The reality of our culture is that we value what we can measure, and we value playing by rules that ensure there's more of it to measure. Costco may have proven it can continue to grow by doing the right thing, but they certainly do not fit the perceptions that regulate the system. When you prioritize intangibles, you risk upsetting the apple cart.

Understanding your customers

The pressures of the business imperative, driving traffic, and the conflict between the value of tangibles and intangibles all muddy the waters of simplicity and make it hard to achieve George Smith's vision. But the most difficult element to manage—one that is crucial to commercial success—is developing proper empathy for our customers.

Even with the best of intentions, if we do not have a systematic way of building a persuasive system designed to deliver a delightful experience, we are limited to thinking about that experience in terms of what *we* would enjoy. While we may be similar to the intended beneficiaries of the experience we seek to create, we are probably not like them in every respect.

In the real world, people do things for different reasons—they have differing motivations.

Many businesses use focus groups and surveys to ferret out these differing motivations, but these techniques often yield artificial results. Participants know they are part of a focus group. They know they are taking a survey. The simple act of observing changes the observed.

Developing and modeling interactivity through empathy is the essence of our story.

It's really not rocket science

On January 20, 1920, Robert Hutchins Goddard suggested to *The New York Times* that a rocket might one day reach the moon.[7] Roundly ridiculed by the public, Goddard was later proclaimed the "father of modern rocketry."

Our own work in codifying Persuasion Architecture as a means of creating and managing persuasive systems is still in the early stages. In identifying the problem and broaching the solution, we're the Goddards of marketing. Like Goddard, we've experienced our share of doubters. Fortunately, those with whom we have worked have come to share our vision, and they aren't laughing anymore.

So let's turn to exploring the specific problems that exist today and start thinking through some directional solutions.

CHAPTER FIVE

Marketers Out of Control

On August 12, 2005, George Silverman, author of *The Secrets of Word-of-Mouth Marketing* and president of Market Navigation, Inc., added an entry to his *Word-of-Mouth Marketing Blog.* He asked businesses and marketers some uncomfortable questions. In his words:

- What if your customers knew more about your product(s)— or, at least, the most important things about your product— than you do?
- What if your products and services were defined by your customers and not you?
- What if your customers were in control of the logistics of purchase: what if they determined how they would buy, where, how frequently, used or new, etc.?
- What if they determined the price?

- What if customers determined the marketing, the messages, the communications, what is said about your products?

- What if your customers—not your salespeople—actually sold the product?

- What if your customers knew your business secrets: your cost of goods, profits, manufacturing methods, finances, etc., or with easily accessible guidance could estimate them with a high degree of accuracy?

- What if your customers knew—if they wanted to—who works for you and their beliefs, interests and quirks?

- If there were problems with your product, what if your customers found out about it in hours, even before you did?

- What if your company insiders could publicly post insider secrets, gossip, etc. about your company?

- What if customer complaints didn't just go to your complaint department, but were broadcast to all of your present and potential customers?

- What if your customers, instead of your PR, determined the reputation of your product?

- What if your customers determined brand loyalty—indeed, the identity and value of your brand?

- What if a few cranky customers could kill your product by badmouthing it?

- What if you couldn't control who retailed, resold or even modified your products?

- What if your retailers could all get together and conspire against you?

- What if your customers made their own commercials, ads, etc. and they got more exposure than those of your ad agency's?

- What if your company were an open book for all of your customers to look into?[1]

Silverman concluded, "Most old-fashioned marketers would be horrified at the thought that these could come to pass. The New Marketers will, of course, realize that virtually all of the above has already happened."

He's right. Up to and including the interactive television experience provided by companies like HSN and QVC, where marketers knew exactly to whom they were giving air time, marketers have controlled the packaging of a product's or service's information, from physical packaging to brochures to media messaging.

That control has never been complete. The reviewing community offered notable exceptions, but even critical reviewers could be influenced. It was still possible for marketing to make its definitive mark on the message.

Today, making that mark is a lot harder. A.G. Lafley, CEO of Procter & Gamble, a successful pioneer in traditional marketing techniques, concluded in 2000 that the mass-marketing model was shifting from push to pull:

> In his first major address since becoming president and chief executive of The Procter & Gamble Company, A.G. Lafley emphasized his company's evolving approach to branding in which "the consumer is boss." He observed that the advertising industry is in the midst of revolutionary change as consumers demand more performance, quality, value and control. Mass marketing is evolving to brand building based on meaningful and individual relationships with consumers—relationships that go beyond product benefits to offer solutions to real and important consumer needs. Lafley noted that successful brands will be transformed into trusted friends and product usage will be broadened into experiences.[2]

That's a problem for behaviorist marketing. How do you ring bells for cats?

Our friend, Mark Huffman, Advertising Production "Dean of How" at Procter & Gamble, puts it this way:

> The mass marketing model is quickly breaking down. It was developed in a time when there were only three major TV networks and far fewer magazines—no Internet, no cell phones, no video games. National advertisers could decide when and how they engaged

viewers by choosing in which TV programs and magazines they placed their ads. The tables, though, have turned; we advertisers are no longer in control, if ever we really were. *Consumers* now choose when and how they engage with us through so many more communication channels than 50 years ago. The consumer truly is boss, and she knows how she wants to be reached.[3]

Today, customers are exerting their control by shaping their own experiences. Digital video recorders allow people to skip through advertisements and altogether avoid shows that don't interest them. This means that even the intrusive advantages of television are waning—people can take what they want and leave the rest. TiVo, a dominant brand of consumer video recorder that allows users to capture television programming to an internal hard disk, is increasing in popularity. It even plans to experiment with searchable advertising![4] Satellite radio offers commercial-free audio programming. And people are blocking online advertising through their browsers.

So where are people turning for their information?

- 41% of shoppers get their information from stores
- 38% from Web sites
- 10% from circular ads
- 3% from catalogs
- 3% from a shopping comparison Web site
- 2% from a recommendation from a friend
- 0% from a call center representative[5]

As of December 2004, 46 percent of all online shoppers started their shopping process through a search engine; 39 percent typed the address of a Web site directly into their browsers.[6] And 176 North American firms with annual revenues in excess of $500 million expect to see significant increases in customer interactions through media-based systems. In contrast, they expect fewer increases, and perhaps even significant decreases, in areas that rely on staff, including telephone self-service, kiosks, retail outlets and call centers.[7]

We would expect this. The complexity surrounding many of the purchases we make in life requires gathering information. It used to be that if you needed information, your options were limited to talking to people or reading a magazine or newspaper review. Now the Internet gives customers numerous options (businesses need to train staff appropriately and get their information into these other formats!).

Word-of-mouth trumps all

Customers can easily get word-of-mouth information online through consumer-generated media—things like blogs, product reviews, and discussion forums. A contact anywhere on the face of the planet is no further away than a cell phone call, a text message, or an online chat. The second Jeffrey leaves a movie theater, he can text Bryan and tell him his Friday night would be better spent not seeing this movie. And that recommendation will trump any marketing campaign for the movie in question.

Even our behavior using media is changing; we're becoming efficient media multi-taskers. It's not simply that the television is droning in the background during dinner; people are often watching television *while* they're surfing online. They are texting while they are reading a newspaper. Lisa's teenage son, Zachary, listens to audio books while he chats with a friend online *and* completes his homework—with no adverse effects on his grades.

When the expansion of information and consumer-generated media is combined with our increasing cynicism, the concept of the appeal to authority grows flaccid. Not that long ago, when a recognized authority offered commentary, it meant something. Today, instead of people being famous for fifteen minutes, as Andy Warhol quipped, fifteen people get to be famous for sixty seconds. If the information looks intelligent and goes into detail (think about those influential Amazon reviews), people do take the source seriously. People we never knew, and never will know, become the experts.

Amazon experiences such an interesting effect that what are essentially promotional techniques like Listmania! (which allows customers to create their own topical lists of favorite products) are now seen as Web site features that involve and benefit customers.

The nature of your prospects

A. G. Lafley hit the nail on the head when he told advertisers that customers want to enter into dialogs with businesses, to establish relationships, participate in the conversations, and be more in control of the exchange.[8] They expect a level of personal communication tailored to their needs and wants—relevance and context are their top priorities.

Through emerging media, the playing field for these dialogs is already in place—and they are taking place, whether or not businesses choose to participate. Businesses that wish to succeed will skip the bury-head-in-sand phase and grab a chair at the round table. It's not simply that you'd like to make sure you were the port of first call; you absolutely need to be sure you package the necessary information in appropriate ways. You must understand the nature of the dialog. You must provide a level of transparency that inspires a customer's confidence.

Taking up your chair requires acknowledging who your prospects truly are because they are now empowered in ways no one could have imagined even fifty years ago. Diverse and fragmented your audience may be, and yet they share certain traits, honed in large part through their Internet experiences.

Every individual actively makes a choice to come to you. They arrive, task in mind, prepared to participate. While they remain engaged in your persuasive entity—be that your Web site, your e-mail, your store, or even your television advertisement—they agree to continue participating in a persuasive exchange with you.

This is critical knowledge: behavior, particularly in the self-service environment of the Internet, is *voluntary, participatory, and goal-directed*.

You can't forget this. People who come to you are interested in you. They are also completely in control of what they will or will not agree to experience. They decide where they will go, how they will engage, what they will spend, whether they will spend, and where they will look for their information.

If your customer refuses to take the next click on your Web site, walks out the door, or forwards past your advertisement, your dialog is over. It is essential to understand that in a world full of options, you are always the equivalent of "one click" away from goodbye.

CHAPTER SIX

Customers in Control

Marketers have always broadcast their messages to customers. Now the reverse is true. Today's customers are broadcasting their intentions to marketers.

This doesn't have to be a bad thing. One of our clients regularly uses feedback from customer reviews on the business's Web site to improve the product descriptions in their print catalogs.

After we made a presentation to another client, the company's senior vice president of marketing assumed we had appropriated a brand-new, confidential market study on which they'd spent both months and millions. He was apologetic and impressed when he learned our analysis was based on words customers typed into search engines. Those customers were broadcasting their purchase intentions clearly with the words they chose to use.

While you are busy "selling," customers are engaged in the related, but by no means identical, process of "buying." Customers need to resolve their own concerns so they can build the confidence to buy from you.

Ideally, they'll build that confidence with information you provide. But if you don't provide it, they'll track it down by going to other sources.

You sell . . .

Your sales process is about *you* and your goals. Customers will engage with your sales process only as long as it provides relevant answers to the questions they ask and helps them accomplish their goals.

Unfortunately, "selling" suffers from the stereotypical image of a sleazy, slick used-car salesman. We don't call that selling; we call it manipulation. Selling is persuading someone to do something. Whether you are trying to get someone to enter a contest, rinse out a used glass, or click through to the next Web page, you are engaged in sales. Money doesn't have to change hands for a sale to take place. But selling is always an exchange of value, even if that value is completely intangible.

To accomplish the sale, you have a sales process. This is the series of steps—some of which may be iterative—you go through as you work toward the "close." Not every sale uses the same sales process, but every sale has a process (some more effective than others). Your sales process is internal. It is *not* about your audience and their goals.

. . . They buy

The customers' buying processes are about *them* and their goals. "Buying" takes place whenever someone agrees to do something. A person is engaged in buying whether he has filled out the contest card, listened to your tirade about dirty wine glasses, or clicked through to the next Web page.

Buyers go through a buying decision process, steps they negotiate on their way to satisfying their needs and achieving confidence that they made the right decision.

Sometimes this process is impulsive and happens in the blink of an eye. Sometimes it takes much longer. Sometimes one person makes the decision; other times it requires input from a significant other. Sometimes five different departments and a C-level executive have to sign off on the decision, making the sale more complex. We discuss the dimensions of a sale's complexity in more detail in Chapter Nineteen.

The two work in tandem

If Lisa comes to your store, your Web site, or your office, she is there because she is engaged in her own buying process—she's looking for a way to meet the need or want that is motivating her. Lisa doesn't care about your sales process, and everything about your sales process should be designed so she shouldn't have to. You should, however, care very much about Lisa's buying decision process.

That inside-the-bottle syndrome we mentioned earlier gets in the way. It's not easy for a business to shift its focus from "us" to "them." It's frustrating to discover that Lisa isn't even interested in talking about a feature you've worked hard to develop. You want her to care about it; you know it's the ideal solution for her. Why can't she see it the way you do? Is she blind? Stupid?

Perhaps. But ultimately, Lisa is the person whose need or want you have to satisfy. She is in control of her money, and her decisions are at her discretion. To meet your needs—your business objectives—you must first meet Lisa's. You have to give Lisa what she needs from you so she's comfortable making her decision.

As much as we would like to script what we want customers to know, they have their own agendas. Those agendas often involve questions that seem silly or irrelevant to you. Or perhaps you didn't think the question would even come up. Or perhaps you were unaware that someone else might be influencing the customer's decision.

In the last chapter, we mentioned the concept of transparency—how much of your business you reveal to your audience (and we will discuss this in greater detail in Chapters 16–17). Today's experience economy demands that you commit to a fairly high level of transparency. It's critical. To feel confident, customers need and want information, and if they cannot get it from you, they'll get it from someone else. It's beneficial to you to acknowledge the substance of what is available, even the negatives, so you can communicate and position it in the proper light.

This version of selling—the non-sleazy, customer-meets-needs-*and*-company-benefits kind—only exists when buying and selling are joined inseparably. At every step, buying and selling must support one another. Buying can never take a backseat to selling.

CHAPTER SEVEN

How Customers Buy

I n Greek mythology, Sisyphus was not a nice guy. He was a murderer and a liar and betrayed the secrets of the gods. After Sisyphus chained Thanatos, god of death, so dead folks could no longer get to the underworld, the irate Hades punished Sisyphus by consigning him to an eternity of fruitless toil (nothing to do with spreadsheets): Sisyphus was forced to roll a heavy block of stone up a steep hill, only to have it tumble to the bottom when he reached the top.

Remove the grim parts of this story and imagine your buying customer in Sisyphus's place. This basic model is helpful to keep in mind as we take a closer look at the customer's buying process and the categories of information you need to consider.

Whenever a customer makes a decision to buy, the final decision reflects the fruits of the decision-making process. The process may take place almost instantaneously or stretch out over a long period of time—but it's a process, not an event.

No matter how long it takes, the buying decision process always begins

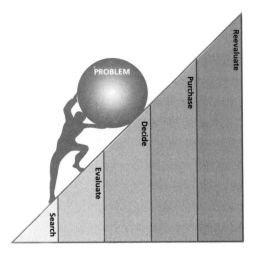

when you become aware of a need. Once you have identified the problem you wish to solve, you begin to search for possible solutions.

While gathering information, you refine and evaluate all the criteria that will affect your decision to buy. You narrow the field of choice to the best few alternatives. You make your choice, then you take action by buying—it's important to understand that deciding to buy and actually buying are not the same. In the final step of the process, you reevaluate your decision based on the results.

Branding and the buying process

The goal of branding is to plant your solution in the customer's brain, so that when the problem arises, the customer recalls your brand as *the* solution. Today, the effects of branding often are diluted. The search for and evaluation of information is no longer confined to family, best friends, business associates, neighbors, or even guides such as the Yellow Pages.[1]

Most sales processes tend to neglect the earlier phases of the buying process. A pressing marketing challenge is to focus our attention on the problem-recognition phase. By focusing on customers while they are framing their problems, we can create the right content and branding messages so we can present the right information for the customers' angles of approach.

In these early stages, many customers may not yet fully understand the dimensions of their problems (especially when it comes to complex, unusual, or undefined issues). This is where we have considerable influence. If we meet the customers' needs through their angle of approach, we are better able to guide the course of their decision-making processes—just like a pool shark hits the cue ball to shape where it goes and what it hits.

Once the customer starts evaluating the best few alternatives in the buying process, we have all but lost the opportunity to frame the problem in a way that emphasizes our strengths and minimizes our weaknesses.

Articulating the need, the want, or the problem

The opportunities for problem recognition and search have expanded exponentially with the growth of available information. It's important to understand and work with how the customer might articulate the situation.

You've got a potential customer out there. How would that customer begin his search? How would he find your product or service? What would he call it? If he has heard of it before, what is his perception of it? If he's looking at your competitors' solutions, how does your solution compare? What are others saying about you, your products or services, your competitors?

You want to persuade this person to become your customer. How do you need to package the information he needs to see? How will you ensure he finds you? How do you influence his perceptions? How will you market to him while at the same time marketing to yet another customer whose needs are entirely different?

If Jeffrey needs to drive a nail, he figures a hammer will do. And if he articulates his need that way, then that's what he will look for. A professional contractor might distinguish between a milled-face hammer or a sheet-metal hammer or a curved-claw hammer or a drywall hammer or a framing hammer. But from Jeffrey's point of view, any of those hammers would do the job. If, on the other hand, Jeffrey needs to drive in a screw, knowing the difference between a flat-head and Phillips-head screwdriver would be helpful when he articulates his need.

If Jeffrey wants to buy a specific book, he'd have an easier time finding it if he knew the author or the title than if he simply knew the topic.

If Jeffrey needs to buy a spam filter to get rid of all his annoying junk mail, it might be helpful for him to know what the filter programs or devices are actually called and to understand the technological implications. He would also need to be able to differentiate between acquiring this service as an individual solution or as an enterprise-level solution on behalf of a company.

If Jeffrey wants to know how to deal with the side effects of a chemo-therapy drug, it might be useful to be able to describe the side effects, understand the nature of the drug, and know all its possible harmful implications.

Perhaps you can see the problem—not all solutions are easy to articulate. The customer may articulate her needs one way; the business may articulate the need another way. It isn't difficult to understand why a customer would prefer to buy from someone who understands her needs by using her terms and "speaking" her language.

The information continuum

Lots of effort has gone into creating a taxonomy of information. But library science isn't very interesting to marketers. It's not a simple discipline; not all information lends itself to straightforward categorization. The Dewey decimal system that works wonders for libraries is useless for hardware. Information exists along a continuum of specificity—things are rarely black or white; there are infinite shades of gray.

Jacqueline Remus of Shopzilla.com explained to us how Shopzilla.com talks about this continuum. They refer to it as a sliding scale that ranges from "compacted information" to "non-compacted information." In other words, the compactness of information isn't a binary function—it's not either compacted or non-compacted. Instead, like those many shades of gray, there are degrees of compactness.

Compacted information. Compacted information is easy to spot. It has unique identifiers, which make for easier categorization. For example, a book has a title, an author, and ISBN. A product may have a model number. These are all unique identifiers. Once customers are aware of the categorization scheme, compacted information allows them to make easy comparisons based on these identifiers. This means they can easily compare a commodity such as a piece of gold, which is measured by its level or purity, to other pieces of gold. They also can easily compare *Ender's Game* at Amazon to *Ender's Game* at Barnes and Noble.

Customers don't make choices based on the compacted information for a product like *Ender's Game*. After all, these identifiers are the same everywhere. The differences that affect the decision to buy—the angle of approach—might include availability, price, previous experiences with the business, and so forth.

Products or services with compacted information are generally easier to sell. However, compacted products can have non-compacted attributes. For example, you can associate compacted information like model numbers, optical zoom, and mega-pixels with a digital camera. But how you would use that digital camera depends more on non-compacted information that affects how you approach the purchase. Are you producing digital studio-quality images? Or do you want to capture your son mid-kick in his soccer game? Which of those compacted attributes—the unique identifiers—helps you choose the best digital camera for you?

Non-compacted information. Non-compacted information usually lacks unique identifiers. If there are unique identifiers, they aren't as apparent. Straightforward descriptions and comparisons are more difficult.

Also, context of the information becomes critical when dealing with non-compacted information. You can easily compact a three-quarter inch nail if you're comparing it to another nail. But that nail is much harder to compact if you are trying to figure out why the kingdom was lost.[2]

When you are dealing with non-compacted information—comparing things like photographers, lawyers, word processors, or aircraft engines—expressing the most relevant features is always one of your biggest challenges.

All too often, the packaging of information fails to address the specific need, want, or problem the customer is trying to solve. In an age defined by its extraordinary amount of information, marketers who want to get noticed need to understand how customers frame *their* questions.

Handles and angles in the buying process

Imagine information as a big blob. You've created some of it. Your competitors have created some of it. Critics and customers have created some of it. Everyone sees the blob of information, but its appearance changes considerably depending upon how you approach it. If you are close up, you can see lots of details that may not make sense to you if you aren't familiar with the big picture. If you are much farther away, you can see the overall shape of the blob but might not be able to discern the details.

How do you grab onto this blob of information?

Customers approach this information blob, seeking both compacted and non-compacted information, from a variety of angles (remember, compactness is not binary—think of it more like a zoom lens). These angles color the customers' perceptions about you, your business category, and ultimately whether she finds you and buys from you.

When customers approach from one angle, seeking compacted information, they use a well-defined vocabulary of unique identifiers. Both you and your customers can completely agree on this vocabulary.

However, when customers approach from a different angle, seeking non-compacted information, they may not use the same vocabulary you would use for describing the features or benefits they want. For example, a family who decides to give their home a new look could be in the market for new furniture, paint, or general remodeling contractors. It's possible they haven't articulated their solution well enough to describe what they are looking for with words that uniquely identify their needs. It's equally possible you wouldn't call it what they call it at any given stage in their buying decision process.

Persuasion Architecture identifies all the angles from which a customer might approach your product or service as well as the vocabulary that could lead a customer to your doorstep (virtual or otherwise).

Persuasion Architecture would also ask what other angles or terms a customer would use in searches and plan Web content keyed to both compacted and non-compacted information searches. It also raises other important questions the customer might not have anticipated: Is the customer looking for a specific feature she doesn't know how to describe? Does she know all the options the business offers? Does she have a proper budget?

Content is developed in response to the various angles from which your customers might approach the information, and it provides "handles" they can grab onto to get the information they want. You may not always be able to figure out the exact angle of approach, but if you provide the right handle—to help customers frame their problems correctly—the rewards are well worth the effort.

For compacted information, the right handle is the set of words you have in common—things like brands, model numbers, and specific features. For non-compacted information (how you describe yourself and your product or service), you need to provide handles that anticipate the nature of the information your customers will be seeking. This is especially critical early in the buying process.

Let's think about a high-level, broad search for a "wide-screen TV" as an example of a non-compacted handle. Our customer is beginning her buying decision process. Her friend has recommended a specific model, so our customer searches using this compacted angle of information—the model number. She quickly learns this particular model is not what she wants.

The results of our customer's preliminary search have changed her contextual framework. This means her angle of approach toward a wide-screen television is different. She may return to non-compacted territory and search again. Or she may search on other more compacted angles that we consider outside our category. She might, for instance, search on "buy a projection TV." How she defines the terms (the handles) will shape how she encounters us (her angle of approach). If we don't account for the terms "big-screen TV" or "projection TV" because we actually sell plasma televisions, we'll lose her as a potential customer.

A fatal mistake in today's marketing world is presenting overly compacted handles. When this happens, it limits the angles through which a customer can approach information. For instance, it took a friend from Wessex, UK, some time and considerable hunger pangs to locate a good "take-away" this side of the pond. She didn't know that in the United States, prepared food that a customer takes with her is called "take-out."

For now, we simply identify the problem. We'll deal with techniques for solving it when we dig deeper into Persuasion Architecture later in the book.

AIDA

The classic business-school model that has influenced countless sales people, advertisers, and marketers is the concept of AIDA, an acronym that stands for Attention, Interest, Desire, and Action. In essence, it's a formula for how you persuade the customer to make the decision to buy.

First, you have to grab Attention—you can't get anyone interested unless you catch his or her attention. Then you have to strengthen Interest, stimulate Desire, and motivate that person to take Action.

We have always added an "S" to this acronym: Satisfaction. Especially in

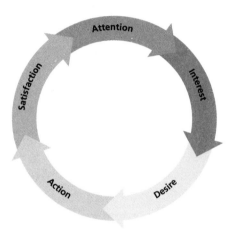

a Web-centric, personal-experience world, the ability to satisfy customers beyond the action itself is essential. Satisfaction is the piece that makes the process come full circle and establishes the potential for future exchanges. Satisfaction *is* the reward. Without satisfaction, the ultimate goal of loyalty is difficult to attain.

AIDAS certainly provides a big-picture view of what needs to take place as selling and buying work in tandem. But the buying decision process is very often iterative. In more complex sales, it's rarely as easy as "I'm thirsty, so I'll buy a bottle of water." As customers navigate through their problem recognition, search, evaluation, and decision phases, there are often different pieces of information they need to know in order to proceed.

Micro- and macro-actions

Our work with business Web sites quickly clarified for us that we were not simply trying to motivate one action. The buying process is made up of many actions. It's easy to understand this if you imagine a customer's progress through a Web site. The ultimate conversion goal of your persuasive system might be to generate a lead, get someone to register or subscribe or enter a contest or make a purchase. But every little step—each click—on the path to the goal is also a point of conversion. You always have to persuade at the level of "micro-actions" as well as "macro-actions."

The essence of the Internet experience is how visitors click from one hyperlink to the next. How they feel about that experience is determined by whether each click fulfills their expectations and needs. Satisfaction with each click (a micro-action) increases their confidence they'll get what they came for (the goal or macro-action).[3]

Every click represents a question your customer is asking. It represents your customer's willingness to stay engaged with you. It represents a unique point of conversion. It represents continued persuasive momentum.

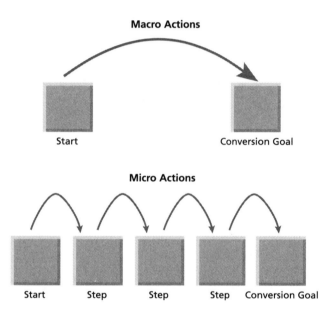

If your customers don't click, communication ceases and persuasive momentum evaporates. If you can't help people get to the information they require to satisfy their questions, why should they bother doing business with you?

Online it's clicks. But every persuasion entity has its click equivalent. When we fail to articulate needs and wants and problems and solutions from the customers' point of view, when we fail to sustain their attention and interest in us, we contribute to an often fatal breakdown in persuasive momentum. Sisyphus's rock tumbles right back down.

CHAPTER EIGHT

Maintaining Persuasive Momentum

Persuasive momentum is a term we popularized to describe the progressive decision-making process that aligns the customer's goals with our own business goals.

If it takes some number of individual micro-actions for a customer to complete the buying decision process and achieve the macro-action, then we need to provide a compelling, persuasive structure around the possibilities that must be available to your customers as they step through the buying process.

You *build and sustain persuasive momentum by intentionally and repeatedly providing answers to these three questions*:

1. Who are we trying to persuade to take the action?

2. What is the action we want someone to take?

3. What does that person need in order to feel confident taking that action?

These simple questions are the foundational building blocks of Persuasion Architecture. Only by mastering these three questions can we align our customers' buying process with our sales process.

When we understand and anticipate what answers, or points of resolution, a customer may require at every step in their decision-making process, we can help them make the decisions that matter to them. These are, after all, the decisions that matter to us and move us closer to our own business goals.

Persuasion occurs when people perceive they are on their way to getting what they want. Persuasion is a forward-moving force. People must feel they are making progress. If a customer feels he isn't making progress, then he isn't persuaded.

Persuasive momentum stalled

Experience #1: Lisa's door knocker. Lisa wanted to buy a new doorknocker for her home, but because the existing knocker is mounted through a metal door, she had to find a replacement with bolts on the same centers.

She fell in love with a particular doorknocker on a large hardware Web site that offered live chat assistance. The item was expensive, as doorknockers go, but it was gorgeous. When she couldn't identify the bolt center measurement from the specifications on the product page, she engaged an assistant:

Celia: "Hello. My name is Celia. How may I help you?"

Lisa: "I'm interested in the Gothic doorknocker, but I need to know some measurements. How far apart are the centers for the bolts?"

Celia: "That information appears on the product page."

Lisa: "Well, it does on some of your pages, but not for this product."

Celia: "Can you give me the item number, please?" (Lisa provides the item number and waits.) "Yes, that item is available."

Lisa: "Great! And the measurements?"

Celia: "This item measures six inches in diameter, and projects $2^1/2$ inches from the surface of the door."

Lisa: "Yes, the product page did mention that . . . and the
          mounting centers?"

Celia: "I don't currently have that information available."

Lisa: "Can you get that information?"

Celia   "I don't currently have that information available."

Lisa: "So who does have that information?"

Celia: "You can call the 800 number on the Web site and ask to
          speak with a customer-service representative."

Lisa: "Aren't you a customer-service representative?"

Celia: "I'm sorry I have been unable to help you today. Please visit
          us again soon."

Lisa didn't call the 800 number and hasn't been back to the business
since. She still has the same old doorknocker.

The persuasive momentum started to deteriorate when Celia claimed
the information was on the product page. Lisa knew it wasn't, and when
Celia offered information that failed to answer Lisa's question, the persuasive momentum halted.

Lisa didn't need answers she already had; she needed Celia to acknowledge her question and provide the appropriate answer. To add insult,
Celia's replies felt more scripted than genuine.

Experience #2: Bryan's Murano. Bryan was 99.99 percent certain he
wanted to purchase a Nissan Murano. He'd done all the market research
online, read reviews, and talked to several friends, but before he actually
made a purchase, he wanted to talk to a dealer about the DVD package
he'd seen online. Naturally, Bryan first went to the dealer closest to his
home. The salesman said the car didn't have that feature—Bryan simply
couldn't get it. The clueless salesperson sent Bryan's confidence out the
window, and the persuasive momentum ran out of gas.

Bryan then went to a second dealer. The salesperson answered all his
questions satisfactorily but kept playing fee games whenever Bryan was
ready to commit to the purchase. The salesman actually had information
Bryan needed to make a confident decision; he just wasn't listening to
Bryan's concerns. This experience was fundamentally a monologue. The

persuasive momentum of the dialog stalled. They couldn't get to the bottom line.

Bryan finally arrived at a third dealer well outside the borough of Brooklyn where he lives. There he told the salesperson what he wanted and what he was willing to pay. Within the hour, he took possession of a shiny new silver Murano.

Bryan's determination kept him going until he found a dealer he could trust—that and the fact he was already sold before he stepped onto a sales floor.

Experience #3: Jeffrey's recliner. Jeffrey, a creature of comfort, decided to upgrade his existing sofa to a reclining sofa. He first looked online, but no Web sites helped him clarify his needs or identify appropriate solutions.

Unfortunately, not every business calls the product a "reclining sofa," which is what Jeffrey calls it. The inability of online businesses to provide direction failed to instill confidence in Jeffrey. But his online forays had given him a better idea of what he wanted. So he turned to his local furniture store. Showroom space in New York City tends to be limited; there simply weren't many reclining sofas on the sales floor. Unable to move forward in his quest, he temporarily gave up.

Armed with the information he'd acquired from sales people and their suggestions that he think about a La-Z-Boy—a name he certainly recognized—Jeffrey later went back online. When he searched on the names of national suppliers, all manner of consumer-generated media complaints associated with the suppliers appeared *before* their Web sites. He was off momentum yet again. And at the time when Jeffrey went directly to the La-Z-Boy site (this has since changed), he was unable to locate a retailer for the brand.

Finally, months later and after countless fits and starts, Jeffrey bought a reclining sofa out of a catalog. It was nice. But it wasn't exactly what he wanted.

Weeks following his purchase, Jeffrey drove right past a La-Z-Boy store on Long Island! Perhaps you can imagine the reaction, "Where were they? And shame on them!"

The acknowledged leader in this category, La-Z-Boy had failed their business objectives in every way. Marketing had done its part; they had Jeffrey's attention, interest, and desire. The persuasive momentum fell apart because of its sales process. La-Z-Boy simply had not made it clear to Jeffrey where and how to take action (the company Web site now includes a "locate retailer" feature).

Experience #4: Another dead-end lead. Our friend, Jared Spool, of User Interface Engineering, told us about a classic case of lost persuasive momentum. One Monday morning, while conducting a retailing test for a client, Spool's researchers met a woman who told them about a two-page Polo ad she'd seen the previous day in the *New York Times Sunday Magazine* (not cheap media space). The only information the furniture ad provided was the Polo logo and the Web address. No store locations. No phone numbers. Just the URL.

This Polo prospect said several furniture pieces "were perfect." She wanted to buy them. Price wasn't an issue. So in their usability lab, Spool's researchers told her to go for it. She did.

She first went to Polo.com, the place to which the ad had directed her. But it had no furniture for sale. Disappointed, she called the toll-free number on the Web site. A polite gentleman, in a most professional manner, let her know he couldn't help her. He dealt only with the Web site, and the Web site didn't sell furniture.

How ridiculous is this story? Sadly, it's not an isolated case.

Maintaining momentum

Recall the three questions that help us create and sustain persuasive momentum.

1. Who are we trying to persuade to take the action?

2. What is the action we want someone to take?

3. What does that person need in order to feel confident taking that action?

At each phase in Jeffrey's recliner quest, a business would want to identify appropriate actions for him to take next and provide the relevant information to meet the questions he is asking at that point in his buying process. Without understanding where Jeffrey was on the path to his decision, a business would have difficulty providing him with answers that were relevant to him.

Many businesses can provide a simple answer to the question, "How do I buy this item in your inventory?" But Jeffrey had many other questions before he was ready to ask that question and heed a call to action.

As we scour about, trying to figure out how to frame and solve our problems, we become like bloodhounds. We try to pick up the scent of an associative trail that will lead us to the information we want. And when that scent evaporates, we begin to lose interest in the trail. If the scent dries up, we disconnect.

All too often it is the build-up of friction that slows and stalls persuasive momentum. The errors and disconnects in each of our stories create friction, much like what would happen if you pressed your foot on the brake pedal to slow your car. The longer and harder you press, the more momentum your car loses, until finally it stops.

The lines between marketing and sales are blurring, especially when it comes to creating and sustaining the persuasive momentum that is at the heart of a customer's experience. Marketers increasingly find they need to incorporate functions that used to be the sole province of sales.

Times have certainly changed.

CHAPTER NINE

Marketing and Sales Collide

While marketers frequently develop material for sales people, sales people usually complain it misses the mark. The best sales people know that a sale is an interactive undertaking. It doesn't lend itself to a static presentation.

Recall that we use "sales" broadly. Whenever there is an exchange of value, wherever you are trying to get your customers to take an action—any action—you are engaged in selling. And you are asking the other person to engage in the process of buying. Sales can be many things:

- The exchange of currency for products or services
- The exchange of personal information for entry into a sweepstakes
- Subscribing to a newsletter
- Opting in to an e-mail list
- Registering yourself

- Agreeing to provide a referral

- Converting someone to your opinion about something

- Inspiring someone to get as enthusiastic about something as you are

- Convincing a child she should clean her room

- A child convincing a parent to allow him to stay up fifteen minutes longer

In short, sales—a word we use for simplicity's sake—is all about persuading people to take the action you want them to take. Persuasion is a transactional process resulting in a change in beliefs, attitudes, and behaviors. Persuasion is the way we motivate people to take action.

In truth, we rarely *change* our minds. Instead, we reexamine old beliefs and decisions in light of new information that influences how we think or feel, and we make decisions based on our reactions to that information. If we ever changed our minds, we simply reconsidered what we knew to be true and how we felt about it. Keep in mind the wisdom of Samuel Butler (1612–1680), who wrote, "He that complies against his will is of his own opinion still."

Persuasion is fundamentally a cognitive and emotions-based process.

Five steps of basic buying

If we were to break down sales the same way we deconstructed the buying decision process, we could describe it as a five-step process. Again, this is simplified for the purposes of our discussion, and it's important to keep in mind that not every sales process follows this exact course. But here are the basics:

1. Initiating the relationship by building rapport and confidence

2. Investigating needs, wants, and problems

3. Suggesting a course of action

4. Obtaining agreement for a decision

5. Closing, or taking action

It's not surprising these steps closely mirror AIDAS, which is itself a sales-oriented perspective on how to influence the buying decision process. The sales process overlaps the buying decision process in the area of investigating needs, wants, and problems. Only in this step are both the business and the customer involved in framing the solution.

Investigating needs is iterative

If we dig deeper into the investigation, we often find that the solution we recommend may be different than the one the customer first imagined.

Lisa wants to mount a wall shelf. She goes into a hardware store to buy a handful of plastic anchors for the job, and finds a range of available sizes. Which is the right size for her job? She corrals a salesperson, who asks her the weight of the shelf and what she intends to put on it, as well as the type of wall on which the shelf will be mounted. With her answers in mind, the sales person directs Lisa to the molly and toggle bolts, which will better suit her needs.

Sometimes what the client initially requests turns out to be something other than what he actually needs. A prospective client calls Jeffrey to ask for help with his Web site's copy, which he believes is the reason his conversion rates are so low. Jeffrey quickly looks through the Web site and discovers that while the copy isn't brilliant, it also isn't the immediate source of the caller's problem. The client would benefit far more from an assessment of his Web site's conversion process for the ads he is running.

Feedback loops are an important part of the sales process; establishing rapport and building confidence are ongoing. They must build over the course of the experience. The level of rapport and confidence that a customer must have to initiate the relationship and begin investigating is not the same level she requires to close the sale.

A sale is a dialog. It depends on interaction. And it's a lot easier to accomplish this face-to-face. As emerging media multiply the opportunities for faceless exchanges and allow customers increasing levels of control over managing their needs, we need to build persuasive systems that acknowledge the necessary dimensions of interaction. These systems have to be sensitive to what the customer is actually telling us. The systems must be able to understand and react to the customers' intentions.

When we reviewed the history of commerce, we spoke of the gradual trend in removing or reducing the friction points that made it harder for customers to buy. We identified friction as the customer's experience of cognitive dissonance, which exists when the customer feels insufficient confidence in his ability to make a satisfying buying decision. Cognitive dissonance usually sets in when the sales process has pushed people beyond where they are in their buying decision process. This is why modeling the interactions is so important.

Unfortunately, modeling interactivity isn't part of a marketer's basic training. In fact, many marketers simply don't live where sales and customer service people do—with the customers. Marketers often lack the "in the trenches" awareness of how the realities of the buying decision process and the customer's needs interface with the company's sales goals.

Marketing is not sales

Traditionally, marketing and sales have been separate and often adversarial activities. Marketing grabs attention, stimulates desire, makes the introductions, and then passes the baton to sales. It's up to sales to carry through.

But the truth is, buying takes place when the efforts of marketing and sales overlap, when both consistently are tuned to and reinforce each other.

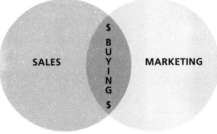

This simple Venn diagram describes our point: one circle is marketing; the other is sales. When the two barely overlap at all, very little buying can take place—the message and experience are disconnected. When businesses are able to increase the overlap between those two circles, they increase the likelihood that the message and the experience will act in concert.

We mentioned in the last chapter that, as the stages for commercial activity multiply, the distinctions between marketing and sales are blurring.

Customers tuned to the value of the experience don't think in terms of marketing versus sales. They couldn't care less how businesses apportion responsibility internally. Customers care about a satisfying, delightful experience. When the experience doesn't mirror the message, they are not delighted.

It is incumbent on marketers to assume greater responsibility, not only for initiating relationships, but also developing them. And every human relationship develops interactively.

CHAPTER TEN

The Design of Persuasive Systems

I n order to design a persuasive system that supports the interactive dialog with a customer, we need to plan for all the interactions that take place across all the different touch points.

Touch points, or what we call "persuasion entities," are the ways businesses make contact and interact with potential customers. These include every traditional and emerging media vehicle you might use, from television ads to radio spots, brochures to Yellow Page placements, out-bound calls to e-mails (auto-responders to full-blown campaigns), Web sites to banner ads, live-chat to customer-service call centers, and any variety of search engine placement you can imagine.

At the micro-level, each of these persuasion entities contains its own little persuasive system intended either to provide the necessary information or provide the momentum that propels the customer to the next persuasion entity. But at the macro-level, each of these persuasion entities is also a part of the greater persuasive system that makes up your combined effort to achieve your business goals.

Push versus pull

Touch points that offer limited opportunities for direct interaction are push entities: marketers broadcast push entities to the customer like ads; marketing pushes the information at the customer. Others, especially your Web-related ones, are pull entities. In pull entities, customers typically initiate the interaction and attempt to pull the information they need from the business.

The effectiveness of all your persuasion entities exists on a slider scale, based largely on where the customer is in the buying decision process (also referred to as a customer's "life cycle"). You need to know which persuasion entity is appropriate for which application. There is considerable art in this, which is why it is difficult to measure everything with the same level of accuracy and detail.

We cannot control all the different touch points that relate to our business goals. At the most obvious level, consumer-generated media falls outside our direct sphere of influence. But even a customer's path through our Web site or store is an event they control. We can influence and persuade, we can manage the experience, but we cannot control it.

Online marketers face these frustrations on a daily basis. They know that customers make conscious decisions to take action—for example, to click on a hyperlink. And yet marketers create systems that are severely limited by a misunderstanding of what interaction means in the context of a persuasive system.

The system challenge

The word itself—*system*—drives many people insane. System-creators tend to be detail-oriented people from technical and engineering backgrounds, methodical types who focus on the mechanics and technologies of the system in a way that is often detached from the business objectives. However, the systems that the best sales people create for their interactions are based on an implicit understanding of customer motivations and behavior.

It is the left-brain, linear, and technology-based approach that usually provides the dominant framework for creating most persuasive systems.

These systems assume there is a causal relationship between what happens first and what happens next, which results in overly simplistic models of the decision trees customers might navigate. This often leads to a form of scenario planning in which the system fails to account for the pieces of information the customer lacks, fails to address the customer's true motivations, and fails to embrace a realistic understanding of how the customer perceives those motivations.

Salespeople who adopt a more behavioral approach wind up incorporating a fair amount of role-playing into their exchanges. They intuitively understand that different customers require different sorts of information, presented in different ways, to help them make their buying decisions. And so, salespeople often have to become the resource the customer needs, rather than being the resource the salesperson thinks the customer should need.

Let's say you go to a brick-and-mortar store to purchase a digital camera. All you want is a camera that takes pictures and isn't a big hassle—you just want to enjoy yourself. You want to know, and truly only care, that the camera is going to fit into your lifestyle. Now, suppose the salesperson rattles on about pixels and resolutions and cabling and any number of other technical considerations you really couldn't care less about in language that leaves you dead cold. If the salesperson can't communicate the information you need to know, in the way you want to learn it, you're not going to be happy. You are going to start tuning out the salesperson. And you'll probably walk away none-the-wiser as well as camera-less.

Now, imagine you've done your digital camera research and inherently understand the advantages or disadvantages of each feature. To feel comfortable about your purchase, you need to know you are getting a camera that will meet your criteria. You want to speak with someone who knows all the facts and can answer all your questions about product specifications. But the salesperson wants to tell you all about how easy the camera is to use and shows you print-out images and explains his Mom has one and loves it. This is going to strike you as vague and ditsy. You are going to start tuning out the salesperson and may well conclude he doesn't know the first thing about what he's trying to sell.

Salespeople are generally aware they need to listen to the customer and answer the questions the customer is asking in ways the customer can "hear." Marketers almost never rely on these techniques.

Under the best of circumstances, there is often a gap between what marketers often envision and what is possible to produce based on the technological possibilities inherent in every medium. Every medium has a role to play, but not every aspect of this dialog can take place in every medium. Limitations are an integral part of the equation—a brochure will never be able to do what a Web site does.

Before we can address how to solve the gaps in interactive communication, before we can create persuasive systems that model relevant dialogs, we need to evaluate the nature of the media and the channels that are available to us as marketers. We also need to understand which data will be most meaningful to us along the way.

CHAPTER ELEVEN

A Web of Interactivity

Our practice grew out of Web-related conversion rate marketing, so people often expect us to exhibit a bias toward the Web as the most important element in the media marketing mix. Many are surprised to learn we actually believe the suitability of the Web varies depending on the business objectives and what's being sold.

For a branding campaign to work, you need reach, frequency, and salience. A good media buy was often sufficiently successful using only the blunter, less precise techniques of reach and frequency. Today, most marketers still use the old broadcast model that relied heavily on entertainment for engagement. Marginal salience was good enough. But now that fragmentation makes reach and frequency more difficult and costly to achieve, salience becomes the critical piece.

What do we mean by salience? Having a quality that thrusts itself into attention is one definition. For our purposes, we also mean something that is relevant.

People evaluate salience at a point of interaction between human beings, when we come in contact with a message or with a Web site. A Web site can be human-like because the experience is dynamic. That means if you think of a click as a question, the place a click takes you is the dialog's answer. This is why you must answer the implicit question associated with a click with relevance.

We turn to a story from Yahoo! Search Marketing to demonstrate the importance of relevance.

Honda was virtually unknown in the pickup truck category when it decided to introduce the new Ridgeline truck early in 2005. With the help of Rubin Postaer and Associates (RPA) and the Yahoo! Search Marketing Editorial team, Honda was able to develop a comprehensive product launch strategy that incorporated direct mail, print ads, television spots, and a Web site. The goal was to increase the association between the Honda brand and the truck category and enable interested customers to get to a Web site for a "test drive" of product information that they couldn't get from other forms of advertising.

To create cohesiveness between offline and online efforts, RPA wanted to work the Ridgeline tag, "Above all, it's a Honda," into their Sponsored Search listing descriptions. Together with the editorial team, they developed different buckets of keywords—some specifically associated with the vehicle model, others simply related to the truck category.

As RPA wrote titles and descriptions for these keywords, they realized they needed to be more responsive to users' search queries—the tag was not necessarily the best means of driving visitors to the site. They altered titles and descriptions accordingly. To maintain maximum control over the brand experience, RPA tailored messages to focus on insider details about the vehicle and bid into the top positions on search pages—so people would see Honda's listings first.

Because only 1 percent of automobiles are purchased online, site visitation was the primary metric used to measure campaign effectiveness. With more than 18 million impressions and over 200,000 visits to the Ridgeline page on automobiles.honda.com, the campaign greatly surpassed Honda's goals. The spike in site referrals from search engines was much larger than the lift in referrals to Honda.com, generated by other forms of advertising. Additionally, the Yahoo! Buzz Index showed a 364 percent increase for the Ridgeline the week after the Super Bowl.

Salience works!

Branding online

The Web is not intrusive. It's very hard to ignore or underrate the intrusive value of sound from a radio or television.

Online, e-mail filters thwart attempts at frequent repetition. The Web is not an always-on sound environment in which someone else controls the programming (unless you are streaming Web radio in the background). People are becoming dedicated users of pop-up blockers. All these factors and more make the Web a challenging place for traditional branding. Today's online branding campaigns, which will certainly evolve in time, are mostly limited to reinforcing existing brands and trying to refine the use of reach and frequency. Most marketers are still concerned with making bigger and better media buys, or trying to enrich experience by using rich media for simple purposes of engagement.

Online branding does attempt to address salience through the popularization of search advertising based on the keywords customers use in their queries. While this can produce results with the potential to be more salient, current practice does not really go deep enough. It usually doesn't target the *intention* behind the query. Salience needs to get much richer and more specific to accomplish that.

Joshua Hay, one of our conversion analysts, shared a lack-of-planning-for-salience example in our blog, *A Day in the Life of a Persuasion Architect*:

Every year my friend Sarah has her birthday around the holidays. Sometimes I get her a birthday present and sometimes a holiday present. This year I decided I would get her something for her birthday. 1-800-Flowers.com sounded like it would be a good place to find a present. I didn't see what I was looking for on the homepage, so I decided to type "birthday" into the search engine.

The search result showed me 182 different items to choose from. On the left hand they had an option to "refine this search."

I figured this was a great way to find the right present. Looking closer, I noticed that this tool wasn't helpful at all. Some of the options presented to me were "Anniversary," "Wedding," and "New Year's." How will these trigger words help me find what I need? If I went to a florist and told them I needed a birthday gift, would they point me over to the anniversary section? Would they ask me if I needed it for New Years? The florist wouldn't ask me irrelevant questions. This year I will just have to go down to the store and get something there.[1]

1-800-FLOWERS enjoys excellent marketing, both online and off. So, even the best marketers regularly overlook salience. They don't plan for it on the granular level we propose.

Web branding considerations

Branding attempts work best for mass-appeal goods and services. Whether we have a strong preference for a particular bath soap brand or not, most of us use soap. It makes sense to brand soap since little else differentiates it. However, branding goods or services that customers rarely purchase is more difficult. These things simply aren't salient in the top-of-mind sort of way.

The Web is best for branding when you want to reinforce relevance and reach customers in the earliest stages of the buying process. If a customer is not yet aware of the brand or is searching for alternatives, then nothing beats the rich information experience only the Web can provide.

Every medium, from passive to intrusive, has a role to play in branding. To evaluate the advantages and disadvantages of the medium, you have to factor in appraisals of where and how to direct effort. Branding campaigns that don't factor in the Web are probably missing the boat.

The Web as glue

The Web is extremely important to the media mix. Why? It functions as the glue that binds all this information. It's a form of connective tissue, like ligaments that allow muscles and bones to work together.

In many ways, the early image of the Web as a monumental resource library is still appropriate. The Web is an excellent place for getting information to people, for persuading them to make decisions and take actions, and for measuring and optimizing the interactions to evaluate effectiveness.

Forrester Research found that "people spend thirty-four percent of their media-consumption time, including both home and work, on the Internet. That's slightly more than the amount of time they spend watching TV."[2] When it comes to marketing vehicles that influence buying decisions, the Web is the clear winner in many business categories (see table below).[3]

Influences on Buying
"Which of the following most influenced your decision to purchase this product/service?"

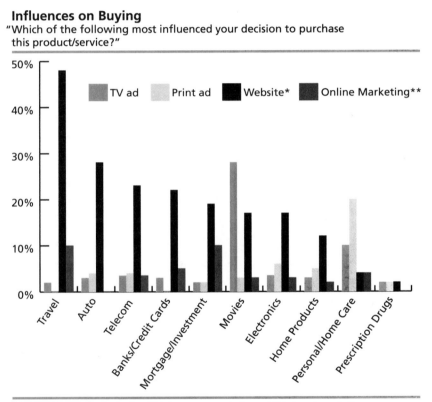

* "Website" includes both official company website and third-party websites
** "Online Marketing" includes web advertisements and email programs
Source: DoubleClick Touchpoints III, 2005

The Web provides a function no other medium can match: It is able to engage with the customer at the earliest stages of the buying decision process. The Web not only provides opportunities for businesses to package information so it is available from all foreseeable angles, it also sets the stage for the quality of the experience promised across the range of a business' persuasion entities.

The simple fact that the Internet makes a phenomenal quantity of information available to the average Joe and Josephine is daunting. How can single voices get heard? Aren't we all suffering information overload?

Sponges, thimbles, and sieves

Amid the hullabaloo over how much information we have available to us today and how thoroughly exposed we are to messaging of every conceivable stripe, it's understandable we would create metaphors that characterize how we feel about the proverbial information overload. We liken ourselves to "sponges" that can soak up only so much and not a drop more. Or we compare ourselves to "thimbles," at which a fire hose gushing water is trained. *Poor sponges (or thimbles)*, we muse, perhaps as we're deleting our 413th junk e-mail of the day while local news on the television plays in the background. How could anyone possibly expect us to cope?

Actually, we cope quite well with incoming information. In fact, we hunger for it. Our brains, thanks to the gate-keeping benefits conferred by Broca's Area, are well-equipped to deal with it.[4] Imagine driving down the same city street every day on your way to work. There are a phenomenal number of details that actually fill your field of vision, but most of them you ignore. Broca's Area has already catalogued them as pieces in the expected pattern. However, when something unexpected in the pattern happens—a child's ball rolls in front of your car, or something new moves in between the bakery and the Laundromat—you take notice.

When it comes to all the information that rains down upon us daily, we're much more like sieves. We filter out the bits that are of value to us or present us with something unexpected, and let the rest wash down the drain. We may coarsen the mesh of our sieves so that more passes through without capturing our attention, but we don't really stop paying attention.

Good thing, too, because there's not very much you can do when your audience is a collection of saturated sponges (or overflowing thimbles) and you want to be the drop that gets retained. But if your audience is a collection of sieves, you can work productively at becoming one of the bits that simply won't wash through the holes.

Doing something unexpected—surprising your audience—will work. But your most effective strategy for staying in the sieve is salience. When you communicate relevance, your customers don't just notice you, they are willing to pay attention.

Relevance rules

Relevance is the piece of the Web equation that everyone seems to acknowledge is important—after all, irrelevance persuades no one. Yet irrelevance abounds in cyberspace. The failure of businesses to identify and provide relevance is one of the top reasons behind the stunningly crummy conversion rates that plague online businesses.

To get a perspective on relevance, let's start at the absurd end of the continuum. Imagine a live chat session between Bryan and a customer-service representative. Bryan is interested in getting a deck-sized outdoor fountain, so he can listen to the soothing splash of water as he works out-doors, wirelessly, on his laptop:

> *Bryan:* "I had a question about the finishes on your Serenity water fountain."
>
> *CSR:* "The sky is blue."
>
> *Bryan:* "Well, blue was one of the finish colors, but actually I was wondering if the finishes would hold up to weather. Can I put the fountain outside?"
>
> *CSR:* "The great outdoors is a glorious playground."

This is the epitome of irrelevance. Put yourself in the equation: If you ask serious questions but never get a relevant reply, how eager are you to do business with this company? Total relevance would look like this:

> *Bryan:* "I had a question about the finishes on your Serenity water fountain."

> *CSR:*   "I'd be happy to answer your question about the finishes on
>   our Serenity water fountain. What would you like to know?"
> *Bryan:* "I was wondering if the finishes would hold up to weather.
>   Can I put the fountain outside?"
> *CSR:*   "With the exception of the blue finish, all our finishes will
>   hold up very well in outdoor conditions."

Now this is relevance! Responses like this would help Bryan feel much more confident about buying one of those fountains.

You think we're being silly, right? Then tune in for some real-life examples that completely miss the target of relevance.

Irrelevance

Experience #1. Lisa is trying to resolve a mobile telephone issue. After dialing Verizon Wireless's customer-service number and listening to the message about how she can handle all her concerns through the Web site, she toddles off to the online arm of the operation, where, unsurprisingly, she fails miserably. So she calls customer service back. At automated prompting, she enters her ten-digit phone number, then her zip code. Eventually she gets a real person on the line. What's the first thing that person asks her? (Hint: It isn't "How can I help you today?")

> *CSR:*   "May I have your 10-digit phone number beginning with the
>   area code?"
> *Lisa:*   "I already entered that."
> *CSR:*   "Please give it to me again." (Lisa sighs and intones the 10
>   digits.) "Now could I please have your zip code?"
> *Lisa:*   "I already entered that too. Followed by the pound key.
>   Doesn't your phone system forward that information to you?"
> *CSR:*   "The five digit code will do."

Not only does this prelude lack relevance, it sets the stage for an experience of adversarial frustration. Lisa concludes Verizon Wireless needs to work on its Web site navigation and integrating its systems . . . until which time it shouldn't be making irrelevant suggestions she solve her problems online! She's also considering trying that other mobile phone service.

Experience #2. Jeffrey wants a Conair lighted makeup mirror for Cindy's birthday, so he touches base with Yahoo!, where he finds what appears to be the perfect pay-per-click ad. It even has "Conair lighted makeup mirror" in bold letters. Enthusiasm runs high as he clicks. When he lands on the company's home page, there's nary a picture of any lighted makeup mirror. Not even a mirror of any flavor. Not even the word *mirror* anywhere in the copy!

Far from satisfying his need for a relevant follow-up on his search query, the landing page drops the ball, terminates Jeffrey's scent trail, and crushes the chance for a sale. At the very least, Jeffrey should have been directed to a category page for "makeup mirrors."

Experience #3. Jeffrey is on Google, investigating the source of his dog's unfortunate bout with diarrhea. He submits the query "dog diarrhea" and gets over 2,400 results along with some pay-per-click ads. One pay-per-click catches his eye and has him thinking he's hit pay dirt . . . until he reads it:

Dog Diarrhea. Huge selection of Dog diarrhea. Low prices, cheap shipping, secure. www.MonsterMarketPlace.com

What has MonsterMarketPlace.com done? They've merged Jeffrey's query with their generic copy. It's a "form letter" pay-per-click. There's no way this is relevant and no way MonsterMarketPlace.com can deliver on the literal promise. And who'd want them to?

Is Jeffrey impressed? Well, aside from the fact this gave us all the best belly laugh we'd had in ages, Jeffrey is not likely to consider MonsterMarketPlace.com a credible resource and click through on one of their pay-per-clicks in the future. This is actually a pity, because if you dredge up the courage to follow the link, you do find some reasonably relevant options.

Experience #4. Lisa signs up for an online dating service and specifies a geographic preference that is admittedly a bit of a long shot. She knows she'll have to be patient to get a match, but that's okay, because the Web site persuades her at every turn that they are really working hard on her behalf to match her with truly qualified people. Relationships take time, the business reassures her. It's worth the wait.

One morning an e-mail from the dating service lands in Lisa's inbox. Due to inactivity, they have put her account on hold. There won't be any more matches for Lisa unless she wants to reactivate her account. She reactivates and then writes an e-mail explaining her situation. She gets a reply; the company says it understands completely and they are on her side. A month and no matches later, the company again puts her account on hold.

Again, she reactivates her account and e-mails a passionate missive— "Honestly, the inactivity on this account is not my fault! Send me a match, and watch how active I get!" She gets this reply: "We understand your situation. I have checked your account and do see that it is active and available for matching. It has been a pleasure assisting you."

The Web site itself was brilliantly persuasive and offered total relevance. But the actual experience completely failed the relevance mission in promise and execution. Lisa's account is now permanently inactive (by her choice), and she's sworn off dating services.

It's not just the producers of content who are scrambling to identify relevance, but also those looking for content. Here, the ability to articulate the exact nature of compacted and non-compacted information heavily influences success.

For increasing numbers of individuals, the Web is the focal point in their search for relevant information and experiences. Relevance is not optional. Businesses must provide it—and that relevance must be echoed across all touch points: cyber, live, paper, or otherwise.

Those "sieves" that make up your audience are developing a growing intolerance for irrelevance; they're coarsening their wire meshes so only the information that delivers pinpoint relevance gets noticed. People typically give you few opportunities to disappoint them, and they judge you harshly if you persist in disappointing them.

Search engines live and breathe relevance

The Web provides an incredible venue for targeting and addressing salience. Google's story should serve as a model to any business that thinks this doesn't matter to customers.

Only a handful of years ago, an unknown search engine company with a silly name went head-to-head with well-positioned competitors. In record time, it became a dominant player. So dominant that "google" became the verb people use to describe the activity of searching: "Just a sec; I'll google it."

Google's success had nothing to do with fancy graphics (it's a pretty stripped-down, dull visual experience). It had everything to do with the fact that Google searches produced exceptionally relevant results. So relevant that the company's "I'm feeling lucky" gimmick, which produces a single search result, is very often right on target!

Search engines have only one purpose: To sort and index relevant content so people can access what is relevant to them. As search engines have responded to the need for relevance, each of the major players today has developed a focus that exists on a continuum of emphasis on technology versus media. Google focuses heavily on technology. MSN relies on both but favors technology. Yahoo! best balances technology and media. AOL has emphasized media.

Capitalizing on salience is an essential part of the equation. If you are looking for a digital camera, results that make digital cameras pop out will be far more relevant to you. And while you might not be directly in the market for accessories for that digital camera, a business can target that associated information because of its salience. If you are routinely reading *The New York Times* articles about interior decorating (the focus of your interest), associated advertisements promoting related resources that otherwise might not be salient to you have increased value. These advertising associations and cross-sells find a comfortable and productive home on the Web.

As customers continue along the path of ignoring overt advertising efforts, content must evolve to provide more sophisticated forms of product placement that not only provide relevant information in context, but also entertainment. There are already Web sites where you can learn more about product placements on shows—especially fashion—and the sites provide links to places where you can purchase the products.

But the true brilliance of the Web lies in being there when the information is required. In the early stages of the buying decision process, many customers turn to Web search as a way to initiate solving their problems. And it is through search that customers clearly and unequivocally broadcast their intentions.

Are you really listening?

Marketers have always claimed, and honestly believe, that they listen to their customers. However, most of this "listening" is carried out in unnatural circumstances—in focus groups or through surveys. In contrast, the Web allows us to *really* listen to customers. They are talking about us on the Web. They are doing millions of searches daily using words and phrases that are related to the problems for which we provide solutions.

The remarkable transparency of the Web allows us to gain a level of intimacy with our customers that is unprecedented. It also allows us to use Web analytics to track and measure many of the dimensions of the interactive relationship that were simply unavailable to us before.

Search is such an integral part of the Web experience that search engine marketing has become its own hot-commodity area of expertise. But search engine marketing that merely tries to regurgitate the words the customer is using, so the search engine's algorithm can find you and put you in a more prominent ranking, is misguided.

The ultimate value in search engine marketing is its ability to help you understand the customer's intent and ensure you present relevant information. Moreover, the value of relevant high rankings is completely undone if you don't follow through on the promise of the result, as we saw in Jeffrey's make-up mirror experience.

Media wars have always been about distribution—getting your information and your product to as large an audience as possible. With increasing media availability, directories like TV guides will become irrelevant.

When you can watch any piece of content that has been created at any time you want, the issue becomes how to find it.

On the Web, marketers have the coveted opportunity to be flies on the wall. There's no way they can eavesdrop on a conversation between Bryan, Jeffrey, and Lisa as they eat take-out Chinese while discussing this book. But on the Web, marketers can pull up a virtual chair.

Online forums, discussion groups, customer reviews, blogs, and many other forms of consumer-generated media are profoundly valuable for their candid declarations of how customers feel about us, what they think about our product or service (irrespective of what we told them they should think or feel), and what sort of experience they had interacting with us.

Interactive companies like the Shopping Channel, HSN, and QVC also incorporate "listening" that influences the presentation of information. Based on input from viewer calls, these companies can redirect the course of a presentation and start to conclude when the number of incoming calls begins to drop off.

The Web is by no means the only medium available in our emerging-media, experience economy. But it is the glue that binds customers' experiences. If our practice is Web-centric, it is because the Web offers us insights and opportunities no other medium can. It allows us to base management decisions on actual behavior rather than on speculations derived through focus groups and surveys.

CHAPTER TWELVE

Brands Cross Channels

Today, marketers are trying to appeal directly to the customer. On top of that, many direct marketers who traditionally have made their appeals directly to the customer are attempting to brand themselves. Dell is an example of a direct manufacturer engaged in a branding effort.

Marketing options range from direct and database marketing techniques that deal with observed behavior to broadcast marketing models that deal with targets. These are not binary choices—it's not either/or. Both direct and broadcast approaches have their place. Today's environment doesn't limit you to one or the other. In fact, in today's environment, you can't afford to ignore either.

Businesses worry about channibalism, "a basic fear felt by many executives and managers that one channel, or line of business, will steal business away from another. There are two facets to this fear: one tied to fears of consumer confusion and loyalty and one tied to managerial salary structures."[1] While customers may prefer to use a particular channel—

such as a catalog or a store or a Web site—in customers' minds, they are interacting with the business, not with the channel.

It turns out that while a company's internal infrastructure may threaten the business's success as a multi-channel entity, channibalism *per se* doesn't exist. In fact, customers who use more than one of a business's channels often increase their purchases overall.[2] And multi-channel customers demonstrate greater loyalty. "With no fear of stealing your own customers from your other channels, the longed-for ideals of effective multi-channel and cross-channeling marketing become a palpable possibility."[3]

To take advantage of the potential inherent in becoming multi-channel means a business has to start thinking like a multi-channel company. Jack Aaronson writes:

> This means unifying customer data across all customer touch points and understanding the brand as the glue that binds the channels.
>
> People are loyal to your company's brand, not its channels (unless you disappoint them). For many Americans, book buying is a very channel-specific task, not a brand-specific task. They buy books at B&N stores; online they go to Amazon.
>
> This is because Amazon was very smart positioning its brand online. Instead of branding itself as just another online store, it aligned itself with the channel. It declared that anything you want to buy online, you can buy from Amazon.
>
> The brand-ignorant were left scrambling to create an online brand that didn't compete with Amazon. This is difficult, as Amazon's brand and product range intentionally overlaps (and overshadows) almost every other online brand. Had multi-channel retailers branded themselves as such, they wouldn't be in the turmoil they're in today. Because brand alignment is usually stronger than channel alignment, B&N shouldn't have lost customers to Amazon . . .
>
> A true multi-channel competitor can offer users an experience Amazon (or any other single-channel company) cannot: shopping over multiple channels (online or off-) in the same environment.[4]

How do customers reach you?

Customers have a number of options for choosing how they interact with a business. The choices they make often reflect the level of intimacy they want with the company. It's probably not an accident that the ratio between people who get their information from stores and those who get their information online is about the same as the ratio of extroverts to introverts in the population (see Chapter Twenty for more details).

Sales favors extroversion; conversions take place face-to-face in stores or voice-to-voice over the telephone. It's a social experience. However, customers are increasingly voting with their mice, opting for more introverted interactions. They are avoiding the interpersonal dimension altogether, or postponing it until they either have no choice or feel sufficiently confident to engage a real person.

Because customers can choose their angle—the channel—of approach, our job is to package information that is appropriate to each channel. Pushing traffic in order to force another interaction doesn't work. Our primary evidence for this? Average online conversion rates today range from the 1 to 2 percent rates of direct mail to the 10 percent rate for catalog companies. Given that online customers are voluntary participants—with *a task in mind*, they come to Web sites *by choice*—these rates are ridiculously low.

Raising the rates

If we were to compare conversion rates between Store A and Store B (brick-and-mortar channels tend to convert about 50 percent of their customers) and discover that Store A's sales were down, we might suspect the problem lay with the salespeople or that something about Store A's sales process wasn't working. We'd hunker down and start examining what wasn't working in the interaction.

We don't usually do this when it comes to other media channels. Instead, we decide it's a good idea to drive more traffic to the channel—even though we know we're sending that traffic into a bucket with some major holes! And so we ask marketers, who excel at driving traffic, to deliver ever-increasing numbers of customers to drive our sales.

Recall our bad-math example in Chapter Four. If a hundred people go into a store and twenty of them buy something, that's not a reason to send *two hundred people* so forty will buy. While sending two hundred people into the store is not inherently wrong, it sidesteps critical questions: What happened to the first eighty who didn't buy? What went wrong in the interaction?

If we look to the people already in the store and figure out how to persuade more of them to buy, we can increase sales by increasing conversions, not increasing traffic. Attention to the persuasive efforts across all channels provides us with a more satisfying and permanent solution that reinforces customers' experiences of the brand as it allows us to achieve our business goals.

Inconsistent customer experiences across channels

Lisa receives an Eddie Bauer catalog by snail mail. She flips through it, sees a piece of luggage she would like, double-checks price and availability online, and then decides to purchase the luggage on her next trip to the mall. A good or bad experience with any one or more of these channels—the catalog, the Web site, or the store—will affect Lisa's perception of *the business* as well as the channel.

Segregating channel responsibility increases the chances for inconsistencies in presentation, messaging, brand voice, and even offer-details across the channels. Inconsistency ruined the persuasive momentum in the first phase of Bryan's car-buying odyssey. Remember how the salesperson told Bryan there was no DVD package for his car even though Bryan had seen the package online? Do you think Bryan's irritation was confined to the salesperson?

Things only get worse when channels within a company have to compete against each other. From the customer's point of view, multi-channel experiences must be seamless. Howard Kaplan, our senior conversion analyst, was shopping with his girlfriend at a Gap store. The pair of shorts she wanted wasn't available in her size—at least not within a twenty-mile radius. Here's what followed:

Gap Girl smiles; she knows the pure delight that's about to follow.

"If you'd like," she explains, "I can place the order for you right now, at the same price we're offering in store. In fact, you can even pay for them with your in-store purchases, all at the same time, on the same receipt. Since you're placing the order from the store, we're even happy to pick up the shipping for you. Would you like them delivered Tuesday AM or PM?"

In this example, the in-store experience complemented and coordinated with Gap's other channels. The customer won. Gap's channels won. Gap won! Unfortunately, that's not always the case.

The set-up for the multi-channel problem often lies in the data we use to help us frame our persuasive processes within and across channels. Are we really looking at the appropriate data?

CHAPTER THIRTEEN

Insights and Customer Data

Companies typically make three types of mistakes collecting and analyzing their marketing data. Some torture the data; some worship the data; some think isolated stories *are* the data.

Torture the numbers until they confess

Those who torture data select and collect only the numbers that confess to their particular cause. Then they engrave them onto a proverbial baseball bat and go about beating those numbers into everyone's heads. Each month, quarter, and year, a different set of numbers beats out the story the business wants to tell.

We have a very research-oriented media company client. Research and numbers are so important to them that, on one of their campuses, there's a 25-yard wall packed with binders, booklets, CD-Roms, and folders full of customer data. Our client's most recent data focus was on what they called "the female decision-maker."

Together we studied the data. We learned a lot about the female decision-maker. We knew her median income. We knew her geographical distribution across the continental United States. We knew what she considered "hip" and "cool." We knew averages for what she spent on different types of entertainment, and we saw that average-spend on a geographic plot.

When we asked our client if they had any data that would reveal "why" these female decision-makers were choosing one entertainment option over another, the only answer was an uncomfortable silence. Our client had identified an important market segment. Perhaps their marketing department was only using the data to support a more "female-aware" marketing campaign. Clearly, the company was on to something, but as we continued our work we discovered glaring holes in their marketing strategy. We also identified marketing objectives that were actually more important for our client to consider.

Our client's real problem was based on a bias for the type of data they collect—demographic data. Because media buys are based on demographic data, it makes sense for businesses to care about these numbers. But demographic data alone don't give you much insight into customer behavior and motivations.

We developed a research project using the Perception Analyzer feedback tool[1] that allowed our client to tie their existing data to new psychographic data so they could explain why customers were buying and behaving the way they did.

O Great Data, will you grant my request?

Then there are those who start a data religion. When all data are sacred, it's hard to decide which piece of data is holier than another. And what do you do if the data seem to exist in some kind of contradiction? Worse, what do you do in the *absence* of data?

Another client, a software company, sells a rather complex business application. Their hunger for data is insatiable. Their sales department religiously collected prospective customer data to score and distribute leads efficiently. The company wanted to "bucket" data based on the company's internal needs. This led to creating a lead-gathering form that asked prospects way too many complex questions. Very few prospects actually completed the form: Our client's over-arching need to collect data completely undermined a critical micro-conversion process. In essence, the company made their need for data the customer's problem.

When we pointed out this offense, we learned our client had no framework for determining the relative value of all the data they were collecting. It turned out a handful of those questions weren't really important to the lead-scoring process—we eliminated those. Others we rephrased to sound less intrusive or to get several pieces of important data with one question.

We helped our client prioritize the data by introducing a simple standard in the lead form application: the only critical data is data that (1) tells us how to communicate directly with the prospect and/or (2) lets us know exactly what the prospect is thinking about.

Let's send Dave

The third type of mistake is when a company doesn't really care about data. They say they have research. In reality, they just sent out Dave (the funny research guy) with a clipboard to ask some customers a few questions.

Nothing against Dave, but we worry about companies that do this. Business leaders in a company simply can't know everything. Well-collected, thorough, documented research is a critical asset in any company's intelligence portfolio. When you rely on anecdotal evidence for your marketing decisions, you are telling the equivalent of ghost stories about customer behavior. Companies who do this can quote numbers and percentages, but if you ask them to cough up a source, you'll hear an awful lot of hemming and hawing.

Hocus focus

Research is most useful when it measures what has already happened. But the most horrific blunders occur when you ask the research to tell you something that no research—not anyone or anything—can tell you. No amount of research can ever tell you *exactly* what people will do. However, well-crafted research should be able to produce data that let you predict what is likely to happen.

Focus groups have been responsible for many a bad prediction. Why? The purpose of many research or focus groups is to get information about what a prospect "might" do. It begins with a hypothetical premise—even the most sincere respondent can't know what she would actually do. This information-gathering technique typically plugs the prospect into an observatory process and asks her to make decisions in a way she never would have prior to your suggestion.

It is simply impossible to recreate an accurate representation of true buying scenarios in a research setting. When a researcher asks, "Which tissue box label grabs your interest more, A or B?" the researcher is engaging the respondent's logical left-brain. Suppose that respondent *never* engaged his logical left-brain when he chose a box of tissues at the grocery store? Suppose he just grabbed the box he "felt" best about? Suppose he only ever grabbed the cheapest box of tissues? Will his focus-group answer reflect his real-time behavior? Probably not. He will behave differently when he's on his own, using his own money, and weighing its value against the array of tissue boxes on the shelf.

Anytime you ask your customers to speculate about what they might like or which this-or-that they prefer, you are dancing on thin ice. Take the New Coke debacle, an admitted mistake in corporate judgment. Coca-Cola truly expected the formula to be a smashing success. Extensive research and countless surveys indicated all systems go. In taste tests, customer after customer preferred the new, "better-tasting" blend. Customer after customer agreed they would definitely buy a better-tasting cola product over their current staple.

Then New Coke went live. The rest is history (and now we have "Classic Coke").

Unfortunately, none of the researchers factored in the emotional connections people have to their sodas. When faced with the choice between a better-tasting cola and the "real thing" they had been drinking day after day, year after year, customers made an emotional choice. It didn't matter if New Coke was logically the superior choice; people opted for the familiar.

Asking customers for their opinions seems, on the surface, an intuitive step toward developing empathy for the customer, and it can be. But you have to be aware of the pitfalls and constraints. Customers don't always know what would delight them because they don't always know what is possible.

On the other hand, surveys are invaluable if you want to figure out why your business is coming up short in delivering a consistently delightful customer experience. If customer-survey data reveals a sudden spike in dirty bathroom complaints, you can take it to the bank that some franchise is not following procedure. As we said earlier, research is great at measuring what has already happened.

Focus groups and other market research can also help marketing teams spot problems with copy or images on a poster or a Web site. They can help you get your marketing materials ready for prime time. But gathering a few outside-the-bottle opinions from qualified prospects isn't the same thing as treating a dozen respondents like mistake-proof business prophets. Nor can these respondents tell you if the advertising campaign will be successful. And isn't that what we all want to know?

Disappointing demographics

Marketers are prone to misapplying demographic data. Because media is sold based on this kind of information, demographic data are often given more importance than they deserve. But mining this information has produced a measure of success in the past, so businesses still turn to demographic data hoping for insight and direction.

Unfortunately, demographics don't provide much useful information about a customer's underlying motivations, emotional needs, and intentions. As an illustration, we'd like you to meet Janet Smith.

Customer profiling

We've crafted illustrative profiles of four women. From a demographic point of view, each "Janet Smith" looks the same. All are college-educated, single, aged 33–36. They are in marketing and have annual incomes of $65,000–$75,000. They all live on the same block on the Upper East Side of Manhattan and work in the same skyscraper in midtown Manhattan.

Each Janet shares the same demographics and the same goal: each wants to attend the Search Engine Strategies conference in New York City. Each Janet decides to visit the SES Web site to get information. But even their mail carrier can tell you they do not share the same motivations, needs, and intentions.

Janet #1. A 36-year-old marketing director, Janet works for an Internet company that licenses data to manufacturers on a business-to-business basis. The company powers comparison channel Web sites and well-known manufacturer Web sites. In addition, it powers all the comparison data at popular industry research Web sites.

Janet makes judgments decisively. She wanted the Web site to generate more revenue, so she introduced the business-to-consumer concept of running the Web site as a profit center. Results have been great. Revenue for channel and manufacturing Web sites is about $5 million. Business-to-business channels generate 90 percent of that, but business-to-consumer is rising.

Janet's main challenge is the inability of search engines to effectively spider their Web sites. She understands a Web site requires optimization for search engines. But because the channel Web sites are dynamic, Janet wants help understanding exactly how to get them indexed. She has discretionary money in her budget to attend conferences but must make sure her assistant can reach her while she's gone.

She has a secondary motivation to attend the conference: She wants to meet some of her favorite industry experts. Deep down, she's really hoping for some good face time with Mr. X, SES's most eligible bachelor!

Questions Janet #1 needs answered: *How can I get my Web sites indexed? How can I get my Web sites spidered? What can I do to optimize my Web sites for search engines? Will there be opportunities to socialize before, after, or during the conference?*

Janet #2. Janet is thirty-five years old and runs Internet marketing for a medium-sized click-and-mortar (i.e., both online and offline) retailer. The company sells products to a niche market, has been in business ten years, and has been profitable from the beginning. Last year, her company finally decided to build an e-commerce Web site. The Web site also offers a few exclusive product lines for testing before they're rolled out in stores.

Janet has assembled a team of energetic young people to develop and maintain the Web site. The Web site ranks reasonably well in search engines because Janet works with the content and IT people to focus more on the customer and less on the technology. But with growing competition, changes in Google's algorithm, and Yahoo! predicted to soon replace Google in its search engine results pages, Janet wants to stay ahead of the curve.

In the past, SES conferences allowed her to network with and learn from search engine reps, industry experts, marketers, engineers, Webmasters, and business owners. Colleagues who referred her to this company were actually people she met at previous SES conferences. She'd like to attend the next conference, but must convince the boss to let her to go.

She'd really like to keep up the friendships she's developed from attending past SES conferences. This time, she hopes to focus more on the conference itself and the organic track in particular. She doesn't want to miss too much valuable information during the morning sessions because of the inevitable late-night parties and time spent with colleagues.

Questions Janet #2 needs answered: *Which of your sessions will focus on organic SEO? What's new at Google and Yahoo!? How can I keep up with their changes? What time do the morning sessions start?*

Janet #3. Janet is thirty-three and is responsible for search engine marketing at an interactive agency. She was recently promoted from media planner to her present job because of her methodical presentation of client documentation. She's still unsure how to get more return on investment from her current ad budget. In her previous position, she oversaw trafficking out ads. Now she has more direct contact with clients and is certain she could manage their ad budgets more effectively.

This year, the company plans to begin marketing to Hispanics. She's interested in an SES session that could help.

Questions Janet #3 needs answered: *Do you have any sessions on marketing to Hispanics? Do you have any sessions that talk directly about search engine strategies and return on investment? What other sessions would be of the most value to me?*

Janet #4. Janet is a 34-year-old public-relations specialist. She partnered with four other specialists and developed a business, writing and sending out press releases that people actually want to read. Because of the experience and flair of the people she works with, she describes her company as the best of the best.

Although Janet's style insures her press releases get read, sometimes her press releases get buried below negative press about the company or product she's promoting in the search engine results pages. Janet wants to provide value to her clients and realizes her search engine optimization skills aren't very good. A creative marketer, she's been in the public relations industry for nearly fifteen years and on the Web since 1996. She's become a household name in her industry. To maintain her expert status, she feels almost forced to learn how to optimize her press releases properly for search engines.

Questions Janet #4 needs answered: *How can I write press releases that will get high search engine rankings? How can I maintain my reputation as an expert?*

Which Janet do you want to target?

If you are responsible for selling this Search Engine Strategies conference, your answer should be, "All of them!"

But consider what you've just read about each Janet. That information gives you pretty good insight into their motivations, needs, and preferences. It did not come from their demographic profiles. Isn't this the information that will help you craft a stronger ad? Isn't this the information you want to use to create an effective brochure?

The demographic data gave you insight on where you could send the information about the conference, but little else. We are not saying demographic data aren't useful—they do offer us a piece of the truth.

Take zip code models. It's fair to say that someone living in the Upper West Side of Manhattan is very different from someone living in Appalachia, so we'd probably be better off marketing our yacht sales to the Upper West Side. But we all intuitively know that not everyone living in either the Upper West Side or Appalachia has the same *modus operandi*.

Demographic data give us an abstraction of who our customers are, as we illustrated in the Janet Smith demographic example. Introducing psychographic data into their profiles clarified their motivations, needs, and preferences.

But even our four profiles above don't give us a complete picture. If we could incorporate some hard facts and data about our Janets, our profiles would be far superior. Imagine how much better we could understand these women if we actually met them, saw their comment cards from the last seminar, or knew what workshops they attended last seminar. In other words, behavioral data would give us the best shot of reaching each Janet with the "right" message and nailing a home run.

In search of relevant behavioral data

Competent marketers crave insight; they want to know what customers are doing and why they are doing it. Marketers depend on all kinds of data to create an environment that will move customers to take action. Of all the data available, behavioral data holds the most promise for creating predictive models of customer behavior.

Marketers use behavioral data to look at an individual's past activity in an effort to predict future activity. Of course, that doesn't mean marketers always apply this information effectively. It's a problem when Amazon uses behavioral data to place children's toys on Lisa's recommended product list because Lisa once bought a toy for her nephew through Amazon. Lisa had purchased hundreds of books and one toy, yet that toy purchase influenced her recommendations for a long time.

The fundamental challenge with behavioral data is that most businesses don't have nearly enough information about the customer to actually predict the usefulness of purchase patterns. Yes, people certainly can make money using behavioral data like this—even the low-budget postcards that land in your snail-mail box offering carpet cleaning or chimney sweep services generate sales. The majority of these postcards are mailed using zip or demographic selects—not anything behavioral—unless, of course, you are talking about "customer" postcards. Vendors mail these to customers who have had prior service and get service every six months—"it's time for your carpet cleaning." That's behavioral, and it works pretty well!

But the true value of the effort falls apart when the persuasive mechanism fails to understand or address the breadth of the customer's context. It is completely *in context* if the customer has shown a history (behavior) of wanting the carpets cleaned every six months. In this case, the customer may perceive the gesture as thoughtful and even a service. The gesture delights. It is completely *out of context* if you are offering mortgage refinances to apartment-dwellers.

Amazon might be able to recommend an author similar to one whose book Jeffrey purchased. It might appeal to Jeffrey, and he might purchase it. Jeffrey purchased Rick Warren's *The Purpose Driven Life*, which is considered a Christian book. He purchased this book because, as a marketer, he wanted to understand what made it such a hot selling book. But, not being Christian, Jeffrey is not looking for books with a Christian perspective. This hasn't stopped Amazon recommending Christian books, even if Jeffrey *isn't buying them*.

Our impression is that Amazon is now considering recency—most recent buying behavior—as a response to the flack they've been getting on the accuracy of their recommendations. Recency is a classic behavioral application with some benefit—it "forces the data" toward relevance by taking into account the customer's recent context.

Modeling persuasive efforts on behavioral data can be a double-edged sword. Behavioral data is very effective when properly applied—certainly tracking behavior is an excellent way to "listen to the customer." While the strategy can yield success, it can also undermine the credibility of the source. Imagine the resources Amazon dedicates to making recommendations to its millions of customers. And yet, it doesn't take too many encounters with a recommendation list that contains nothing of interest before you simply start tuning out that noise.

How people buy and what to do about it

At the end of the day, commanding the information that tells us how people buy and what we should do about it is a Holy Grail. It's why we started our company. It's why you are reading this book.

Market data is only of value if it can give us better insight into how and why people buy. When conducted properly by highly skilled statisticians, market research can even be used to predict certain types of behavior patterns in very controlled situations. Election pollsters have an extraordinary track record in forecasting election results.

In the case of our media company client—the one interested in the "female decision-maker"—the premise was pretty simple. If we could accurately "bucket" people by psychographic segment, we would begin to see patterns of behavior emerge.

The Perception Analyzer consultant who compiled the data for us was very excited after the first day of research. He made some interesting observations: he had noticed specific patterns in how different psychographic segments chose to respond. He pointed out that one group was very decisive—they took strong stands and gave firm answers. Another group was more conservative and responded to questions in a slow, quiet, careful manner. He was tickled to find out these patterns mirrored the preference patterns of a corresponding psychological temperament (we'll dig into this in Chapter Twenty).

Our software company client—the one with the complicated lead-generation form—needed a clear framework for determining what information was most important to their business goals. When we improved their framework for collecting data, we improved their lead flow dramatically.

Both companies have reams of market research data. And they are smart companies. They are leaders in their respective fields. Yet they didn't fully grasp the practical and profitable applications for their data.

Companies still are digging relentlessly for answers in their demographic data and winding up disappointed. Companies still are grasping at focus groups, surveys, probability studies, and other misused and abused data-gathering techniques, despite their horrible track record, hoping this research will be the magic crystal ball that offers a drop of validation.

And what do you do if you just don't have access to research? What if your company is either too small or too new to be able to probe anything meaningfully? Do you stick a moist finger in the wind?

Research can, and often does, answer questions, but it can only answer the right questions if you ask them properly. And that's never as easy as it looks.

Actually, we don't really want better research. We want data that will help us create predictive models of scenarios that people will engage in. We want to be able to ascribe the customer's place in the buying cycle to those predictive models. And we *must* be able to relate that observable behavior to a balance sheet, cash flow statement, and/or the profit and loss statement.

Is all of this even possible? Yes.

Time for a new framework—Persuasion Architecture

We've identified lots of problems and challenges. Maybe you can relate to some of them. Maybe you've found yourself in violent agreement with us. Maybe you have even found your own solutions to these problems. Heck, you might even be an expert in solving one or two of these problems!

Maybe you've experienced a data challenge we haven't described here. Have no fear. We're not done defining challenges yet.

In our work helping clients market online, we've found ourselves constantly taking bits and pieces from one discipline and applying them in another with tremendous success. Everyone's business and marketing challenges are unique, but there always seems to be a well-established solution, often in an unrelated business model or discipline.

We began creating systems using principles we learned from the medical field, from construction, from science, from psychology, and of course from architecture. We took a more holistic approach to solving our clients' challenges—we wanted to cure the entire problem, not simply put a Band-Aid on the cuts of ineffective marketing.

We saw the need for a methodology that would serve as a dynamic framework, something anybody could use to leverage all those best principles and shape the persuasive process in an increasingly complex, interconnected marketplace.

So quietly, while dot-com bubbles were bursting and everyone seemed to be giving up on the Internet, we were jumping in with eyes wide open, armed with our newborn methodology called Persuasion Architecture.

From this point on, we begin tackling the problems in light of their solutions. In the next chapter and beyond we reveal how we have successfully applied Persuasion Architecture to solve and manage marketing's challenges.

CHAPTER FOURTEEN

Personalization or "Persona-lization"?

I t feels wonderful when a business treats us as if we were special: When the waiter knows we like our iced tea with so many lemons that they slide off the table onto the floor—and always makes sure we have that many lemons. When the woman in the dress shop sets aside a new arrival, in our size, because she knows it's something we would love. When the bartender knows our favorite beer and starts pouring as we walk in. When the hotel knows we like king-size beds, firm pillows, and chocolate-chip cookies and has them waiting for us every time we stay there.

When someone acknowledges us as individuals and personalizes our experience based on our unique characteristics, we feel understood and valued. Our feelings of good will increase. Our confidence grows. Even our tolerance broadens. Personalization casts a powerful spell. Marketers understand this.

When the Internet and its legion of related technologies began the rise to fame and greatness, many a red carpet commentator touted the promise of better personalization and tailored customer experiences. Pies were served in every corner of the sky.

It would be sublime if every business could provide each and every one of their customers with truly personal personalized experiences. In fact, 80 percent of customers say they want a personalized experience.[1]

Too personal?

Personalization sounds great, but there is a problem. Sixty-three percent of the people who want a personalized experience don't want to give up the personal data that would make it possible.[2] And privacy concerns are only increasing. Just imagine the world of *Minority Report,* that film with Tom Cruise, where ads are personalized by your biometrics. Do you want merchants accessing your thumbprint and retina scans?

So what's a business to do? Read minds or tea leaves? Supply mood rings?

Online and wireless media may offer faceless exchanges, but the customer on the other end of a device isn't thinking about the thousands of other nameless individuals interacting with you at that precise moment. She's engaged in a one-on-one experience; she's focused on the dialog she's having with you. And to her, it's already personal.

One of the obstacles impeding the promise of personalization is that personalization involves a level of commitment the prospective customer may not have and may not even want. Personalization aimed at acknowledging how we go about meeting our needs requires us to share intimate details with strangers through media we often perceive as risky.

And of course, not every customer comes at the experience from the same angle—different people feel differently about what constitutes personalization. Not everyone wants to view information the same way.

Businesses already invest heavily in personalization processes. They set up database merges so their e-mail greetings open with, "Hi Bryan!" They offer options that allow customers to enter and store shipping and billing information, track their orders, review their account status, customize their e-mailing preferences, even create virtual models for trying on clothes online.

Customization vs. personalization

Customization and personalization are two related but different processes. Customization takes place when the customer takes control of his experience with your brand, your products, or your services. He customizes his experience by modifying the parameters of his expressed terms—if you let him.

Personalization takes place when the brand takes the lead in shaping a presentation or product or marketing piece on behalf of the client. So, while we can make a stab at allowing the customer to customize his experience through various application tools, we require huge amounts of information to offer a truly personalized experience.

Both of these approaches can be valuable to customers, but they still fall short of what constitutes meaningful personalization when the customer is engaged in the buying process.

Personalization overkill

Personalization efforts are really nothing more than specific, sophisticated attempts to segment your marketplace. Almost everything marketers do is an attempt at segmentation.

One-to-one marketing is a popular idea in some marketing circles these days. Its premise is that technology will soon offer us the possibility of creating personalized messages or a dialogue for every prospect throughout the buying process. On the surface, it sounds exciting. But if you think about it, its true value becomes elusive. The buying cycle in many categories is simply too long to make reusing this level of personalization worth the investment. Not every business benefits from frequent repeat customers. How often do you build a new house, hire an attorney, or choose enterprise software?

In addition, not all segments are created equal. Eventually the marketing costs for such a massive undertaking would outweigh its ability to contribute to revenues. It would be marketing overkill, too much of a good thing.

"Persona-lization" delivers

For marketers, the promise of personalization is not the end. It's only a means. What marketers really want to achieve with personalization is accelerated customer intimacy. The solution to this problem, however, is not personalization or even customization. These things may or may not add any real value to the selling process.

The answer is "persona-lization."

We will spend much more time with personas when we talk about creating and managing persuasive systems, but for now, think of a persona as an archetype, a representative of a typical segment of your audience. Although we develop personas as fully fleshed-out characters so you can identify and empathize with them, they essentially represent the different modes customers exhibit when they interact with you. Personas are stand-ins for the various angles from which your customers view their problems and your solutions.

When we allow every potential advertiser and business to know all our personal preferences in intimate detail, we risk opening Pandora's box. It's a familiarity few of us want to share. Persona development lets businesses capitalize on a level of familiarity that is a significant improvement over the personalization techniques they currently use. We don't doubt that as our collective experience working with personas matures, we will continue to see their potential blossom. Personas give you an in-depth, personal glimpse at your customers and their personal preferences without having to ask every customer to divulge that in-depth, personal information.

"Persona-lizing" also honors the nature of how relationships develop. Imagine a young gentleman asking his blind date what sort of lingerie she prefers even before they've met in person. The relationship might get to the point where he could ask her lingerie preferences, but earlier in the courtship it would be more appropriate if he asked whether she preferred Thai to sushi or a comedy film to a rock concert. Human relationships unfold in particular ways, and you can't reach for intimacy without establishing some foundations.

When we feel understood and valued—something a business can never accomplish merely through greeting us by name—we are far more inclined to reveal more about ourselves. "Persona-lization" over personalization simply acknowledges the priorities in our mission to speak to customers in language they appreciate about what matters to them.

When personalization occurs within a persuasive system, it is far more effective if it is expressed in the context of "persona-lization," where the customer identifies himself through his observable behavior rather than by having to provide specific details.

Knowing Lisa is female generally tells you much more than knowing she is forty-eight. A forty-eight-year-old person isn't exempted from participating in things that twenty-one-year-olds or sixty-seven-year-olds enjoy. Because she is female, you could assume she won't be looking to get a prescription for Viagra. But she might be interested in Viagra on behalf of a significant other. The experience you'd create for a woman in this case would have to be very different from the experience you'd create for a man.

Further, personalization cannot reach beyond what it is reasonable to assume. The fact that Bryan purchased a book of Emily Dickinson's poetry is more personalized information than knowing he simply purchased a book. You can't abstract an interest in Emily Dickinson's poetry from any other data. You don't have any idea why he had that particular interest, and you can't reasonably expect Bryan to buy anything else written by Dickinson.

"Persona-lization" can feel very personal

Jeffrey is an avid reader, and he always wants more books than his budget will accommodate. He's concerned he'll miss out on a great book, and that the book he *really* wants to read will remain abandoned on the bookstore shelf. We doubt Jeffrey's alone in wanting to get just the right book, so in him we have the makings of a specific persona with an identifiable shopping mode.

It wouldn't be difficult for a bookstore to shape an experience that would delight the Jeffrey persona. Management could install a few comfy chairs and sofas, maybe a coffee bar—create a setting that allows him to take his time selecting, letting him dip into the books so he can settle on the "right" one.

Even better, if the store offered a "Buy four, get the fifth free" deal, Jeffrey wouldn't have to winnow his choices; he could walk out with all of them. This is a more personalized experience for Jeffrey, yet the store doesn't need much personal information about Jeffrey to provide it. They can achieve it through a "persona-lization" technique.

The segment game

Marketers segment prospects. It's part of the game. We segment our audience so we can assess which customers are most valuable to our company. We segment our audience so we can gain insight into how to market to our customers or even *whether* we market to them.

A bookstore might determine that Jeffrey-type customers are its least profitable segment. It can then decide whether it wants to increase the value of Jeffrey-types or whether it would prefer to strategically remove them from the company's marketing efforts.

The angles of approach customers demonstrate through their behavior can reveal extraordinary insight into the mode in which they are operating. Ultimately, knowing the behavior is more valuable to the interaction than knowing detailed personal information about a customer.

It is almost always more effective to "persona-lize" before you personalize.

CHAPTER FIFTEEN

Introducing Personas

per·so·na *n.* (*pl.* **per·so·nas** or **per·so·nae**)[1]

1. A voice or character representing the speaker in a literary work

2. The characters in a dramatic or literary work

3. The role that one assumes or displays in public or society; one's public image or personality, as distinguished from the inner self (Jungian psychology)

The dictionary definitions of persona are revealing. Personas are characters; they have a voice, they are representations or stand-ins for somebody else, and they play a role that, while connected to, is also distinct from their inner selves. They are images, personalities.

Of the people who actually try to use personas, most think of personas as representations of market segments or user groups that are based largely on demographics. Frankly, it's easier this way. But as we've seen, the results offer a thin porridge when we're looking for hearty stew.

Some businesses are starting to use personas and conceptualizing them as communication tools, but most applications are still limited in their perspective. Best Buy, in particular, has experimented with personas based on relational and transactional customer models, and "Jill" has become their "soccer-mom" persona who allows in-store employees to empathize with women customers who lack technical savvy. Best Buy even has created specific Jill stores. (We'll revisit Best Buy in subsequent chapters.)

Nobody currently uses personas the way we do. For us, personas are stand-ins for buying modalities. These modalities allow a client to understand every possible angle from which a customer can approach and engage with information. They help a client package that information to maximize its relevance to the customer's context.

As marketers, what we really want is to build persuasive systems that acknowledge *modes* of behavior (as opposed to simple *patterns* of behavior), information-seeking habits, and decision-making styles. Individuals in demographic market segments can move from mode to mode, even within a single interactive experience. It's similar to the problem we encountered in predictive personalization: buy a gift for someone who isn't at all like you, and that throws off your recommendation results.

This is important, so we'll say it again. *Personas are representative stand-ins for the modes in which it is possible for individuals to interact with you and your business.* The focus on buying modes in "persona-lization" addresses the motivations and needs of your audience far more meaningfully than demographic segmentation alone.

When it comes to meeting needs, we all consider ourselves unique. Part of the appeal of personalization depends on the appearance that a business acknowledges us as unique and special. And it goes without saying that when you speak to an average, you are not speaking to the vast majority of your audience. Personas are based on typicals, not averages.

If we were to assign priorities to our personas, we might understand these weights in terms of the market potential the persona represented. For those business categories where it's easier to figure out market size and distribution, like automobiles, we could ascribe a valuation and prioritization to the scenarios these personas will engage in. For example: a scenario where a person is evaluating alternative SUVs (higher margin business) might be more valuable than a scenario where a person has decided to buy a compact car (lower margin business) and is now shopping around only for price.

Another example: If we had a magazine subscription Web site and knew each typical segment, we could ascribe a market value to each segment. We might also know there were many more buyers of news magazines than buyers of knitting magazines. Thus, if there were a conflict in presenting the view we want the customer to have, we could rank our views because we know the value of each segment. In this case, we'd give the news magazines priority.

Many businesses have heard the word "persona" before. As the Internet experience has blossomed, the word has been associated with marketing, Web development, and especially with design and usability in the medium. Because it is a familiar word, we chose to use it. But the way we advocate using personas differs considerably from the way businesses currently use them, although if you combined all available ideas about what a persona is, you'd come close.

We started using the word intentionally in 2002. We had come to our understanding of the powerful marketing and sales role of personas by working with a model that was more complicated and abstract, and therefore more difficult to convey, than the more limited models that then prevailed. Our model examined the question of modality—the critical modes of information-gathering and decision-making a customer brings to the interaction—through three different filters.

Let's look briefly at these three filters. We will dig much deeper into them in subsequent chapters.

Topology

The most important of our filters is topology. Every business has one, literally a lay-of-the-land that defines the characteristics of the business and differentiates it from other types of business. Digging beyond the surface, we realize topology ultimately addresses the lay of the competitive landscape; all businesses exist in context, not as stand-alones. Every business has competitors, both explicit and implicit.

Topology reveals the specific angles of information a business possesses. Even innovations have competitors for angles of information, if only for the mind space that the problem and old solution occupy. You might devise an incredibly innovative product that solves a problem in a way no one ever considered before. You have no identifiable competitor for this product. And yet you still have to ask questions about your competitive landscape. If the product solves a problem, then how did people solve this problem before you came along? Even if the answer to this question is that people have simply ignored the problem, the answer shapes your specific angle of information.

It may be painfully obvious to say people don't buy bubble gum the same way they buy computers, but the particulars of this dynamic— Why don't they?—are always the first things we need to examine and understand.

Psychographics

Our second filter for understanding modality is psychographics. The fields of psychology, personality, and even consumer psychology are vast areas of inquiry. Each of us is as unique as our thumbprint or our DNA. However, the thought of devising a persuasive system that could uniquely address billions of individuals is daunting, not to mention cost prohibitive given current technology.

The good news about our personality preferences is that, for all our individuality, the ways in which we relate to the world, gather information, make decisions, and act upon those decisions are not wildly unique. We all fall into a limited number of categories of personality types. Centuries of studying human behavior have recognized that human beings have an "operating system" related to the bilateralism (right and left sides) of the brain. (We'll discuss this in more detail in Chapter Twenty.)

Psychographics isn't limited to the human operating system; it also embraces the lifestyle choices people make. In this respect, it provides a valuable merger with behavioral dimensions. When you combine what motivates people with what people are interested in and actually do, you dramatically improve your ability to model predictive behavior paths.

In terms of predictive ability, behavior usually trumps psychological preferences. If you've bought ten pieces of expensive jewelry in the last year, you are likely to buy more in the future. If you've purchased Harley Davidson accessories before, you'll probably purchase some again. If you subscribe to *Snowboarder* magazine, we can assume, regardless of your demographics or any supporting behavioral data, you will be interested in products and services associated with snowboarding.

Our colleague Jim Novo tells a story of his experience at HSN. It was conventional wisdom at HSN that the best customers were women fifty-five and over. Jim and his metrics gang decided to turn the actual data inside out and backwards, sort of like playing with a Rubik's Cube.

The results surprised them. Over 20 percent of the best customers were under thirty. In searching for an explanation, they discovered what their best customers really had in common: all these people watched lots of television. Women over fifty-five are the heaviest watchers of television, but there was also a substantial audience of under-thirties, young affluent people who also had extra time on their hands. So HSN began relying less on the demographic identifiers—age and income became a little less important in their modeling—and refocused on television viewing patterns.

When you are focused only on acquisition, actual behavior is difficult to target. You simply don't know; you don't have any data. Psychographics that rely on lifestyle and personality preferences are all you have to work with. When you combine personality preferences and lifestyle choices with behavioral data, you have the makings for a remarkably robust predictive model.

Demographics

The last in our trio of filters affecting customer modality is demographic data. Some of these data have a direct impact on how we go about defining personas. But we need to be clear about what demographic data can actually help us accomplish.

Demographics tell us where we might find the people who might buy our stuff. They tell us about various limitations in our audience so we can accurately define our universe of buyers. Babies can't throw darts. Men can't have babies. There are no teething sixty-year-olds. You don't need automatic car starters in Florida. Demographics do have something to tell us about which people will buy what.

Demographics are also of value in helping us create personas because they offer us a degree of precision in describing each persona. Demographic information helps us flesh out a persona, making that person a more real and more recognizable customer. This lets a business develop empathy with its audience. In other words, the more a business knows about its personas, the better it can understand and relate to them. They feel like real people. It is always easier to imagine yourself having a dialog with a flesh-and-blood person rather than a cardboard cutout.

Our use of personas is more akin to writing scripts for interaction than to designing interfaces as Web developers do or designing product campaigns as marketers do. Once we have compiled the right information about our personas, we use them to generate empathy within the business for the persona's wants, desires, needs, and problems.

When we understand and empathize with our customers, we can better predict what information they want, when they want it, and how they want it delivered. We can create scenarios that describe how these customers will want to interact with us. Those scenarios, in turn, provide us with a solid foundation for monitoring, measuring, and optimizing our persuasive system based on what we've predicted in the persona creation process.

To connect with your customers, to speak their language, to understand their needs and motivations, you must first empathize with them.

Empathy: rewriting the golden rule

"Want some toast?" Lisa asks Bryan.

"Sure," Bryan replies.

Lisa serves up two plates of toast prepared just the way she likes it: lightly toasted, golden brown, and chewy. Bryan eats the toast and says thanks, but he isn't exactly delighted, because, as he explains, he happens to prefer his toast dark and crisp. Who knew?

You've probably heard the saying, "Do unto others as you would have them do unto you." The problem with the golden rule is that *we* become the yardsticks against which we measure the needs of another.

Obviously not everyone wants the same things or wishes to be treated in the same way. The loss of the "mass" in mass marketing through increasing fragmentation of audiences into niche alternatives only reinforces the strength of voices clamoring to have it their way. Yet lots of businesses, in no small part because of inside-the-bottle syndrome, persist in setting up processes in ways *they* understand and in ways *they* find appealing, as if the businesses themselves were their own, sole target audience. You can imagine the extent to which you limit your persuasive potential when you focus on what you want rather than what your customer wants.

When we are sensitive to the quality of our relationships, we discover we truly delight people when we treat them as *they* would like to be treated. Of course, this requires empathy and a willingness to walk in another's shoes. David Keirsey, an investigator of human temperament and author of *Please Understand Me II*, speaks to the need for this level of compassionate understanding:

> If I do not want what you want, please try not to tell me that my want is wrong . . .
>
> I do not, for the moment at least, ask you to understand me. That will come only when you are willing to give up changing me into a copy of you.
>
> I may be your spouse, your parent, your offspring, your friend, or your colleague. If you will allow me any of my own wants, or emotions, or beliefs, or actions, then you open yourself, so that some day these ways of mine might not seem so wrong, and might finally appear to you as right—for me.
>
> To put up with me is the first step to understanding me. Not that you embrace my ways as right for you, but that you are no longer irritated or disappointed with me for my seeming waywardness. And in understanding me you might come to prize my differences from you, and, far from seeking to change me, preserve and even nurture those differences.[2]

The persuasive effectiveness of applying this "rewritten" golden rule—do for others as they would like it done to them—is the most compelling justification for designing with personas. When you can completely empathize with your customers, when you can interact with them in ways that are meaningful, emotionally engaging, and persuasive to them, everyone wins!

The "emotional future"

Saatchi & Saatchi CEO "guru" Kevin Roberts recently delivered a key note address in which he emphasized, "The advertising business has become a place where 'there are no rules, there are no formulae, there is no best practice' and nobody has a clue about how to effectively market products to the masses . . . 'The future belongs to those who can make emotional connections in the market' . . . The idea is that 'you've got to be entertained as well as informed.'"[3]

In Roberts' estimation, the new age of marketing will depend on "sisomo," the combination of sight, sound, and motion as experienced on digital screens that allow advertisers to articulate the truisms of "a good story well told, emotion, humor, and music." Most of the money we spend on communications, he claims, is "money down the toilet that's completely wasted because it [is] based on rational, reasoned information that consumers are just letting it go wang! wang! wang! right past them. They don't care. The winners in the attraction economy will be those who get to that emotional future first and fast."[4]

We can agree with Roberts that incorporating sensory elements into messaging is a powerful way to capture attention—sight and sound have the ability to activate Broca's Area in our brains, and Broca regulates what gets noticed. But creativity for its own sake is wasted effort if it does not deliver a relevant message.

Remember Nissan's GI Joe, Ken, and Barbie TV ad? The one where Barbie ditches Ken and drives off with GI Joe in a hot red car (van Halen pulsing in the background)? It constituted one of the most famous ad campaigns in the last fifteen years. Bummer for Nissan, though. They spent over two hundred million dollars, and sales actually went down. How come? Not many people are persuaded to invest $35,000 in a substantive product like a car based on style alone. The creative was so overwhelmingly captivating and entertaining that most people couldn't recall the manufacturer's name, let alone the fact they were car ads. Nissan learned the hard way—these days they're focusing on substance, an issue that's more relevant to their audience.

Laura Ries, president of the marketing strategy firm Ries & Ries, often comments on branding blunders and their unexpected consequences. Advertising that focuses on creative entertainment at the expense of relevance offer little more than endorsements of the icons around which the branding is supposed to take place. Thus the classic flops. There's Mr. Six of Six Flags: "While the Mr. Six ads have been the bomb, attendance at Six Flags has flopped. Attendance figures are down four percent from last year."[5] In similar fashion, there's Joe Isuzu for Isuzu, Sock Puppet for Pets.com, Priceless for MasterCard, and Spongemonkeys for Quiznos. All got lots of attention, and all failed to deliver the goods. We know the Taco Bell dog sold many more Chihuahuas than it did tacos or burritos. And in 1987, "the claymation California Raisins, with a little help from Ray Charles, moved more licensed raisin merchandise than they did actual raisins."[6]

It's not just the high-profile creative winners that fail to deliver. Some industry observers identify Gap's celebrity-endorsed, MTV-like advertising as the leading culprit for the company's three years of increasingly poor sales performance. They claim, "It is basically a statement that we have no meaning, relevance or value of our own, but if we stand next to someone real close, maybe some of it will wear off on us."[7]

Jeff Hicks, the creative person of the perhaps too entertaining Burger King "Subservient Chicken" campaign and CEO of Crispin Porter + Bogusky, makes the following claim:

> Irrelevant engagement on the Internet is no different than irrelevant engagement on television. I've had engagement with an ad for adult diapers, and that's totally irrelevant to me . . . Forward-to-a-friend is nothing more than an awareness generator. There's no guarantee that your sense of humor or your needs are relevant to this. I am a huge believer that great marketing has to engage.

Obviously, great advertising has to engage. But engagement doesn't guarantee relevance.[8]

Reinforcing that "outcomes are not conversions," Rebecca Lieb, Executive Editor of the ClickZ.com Network, concludes that "engagement is, at present, a pretty flabby goal, marketing-wise."

All this delirium about engagement calls to mind a former student of mine who came racing in one morning, deliriously happy and sporting a ring. Breathless, she shared her good news: she and her boyfriend had become engaged the night before. After making the proper congratulations, I asked if she'd thought at all about a wedding. Her face fell. "Wedding?" she asked, incredulously. "There's not going to be any wedding. We're just . . . engaged."[9]

Engagement as an end unto itself is not enough. Clearly something beyond the simple entertainment value of the message must enter the mix.

The role of emotion

We would also agree Roberts, the "sisomo" advocate, was getting closer to identifying the essential need when he mentioned "the emotional future." It is true that people rationalize the decision to buy based on facts, but they make buying decisions based on emotions.

Identifying and speaking to the emotional needs in your audience has very little to do with being emotive. It's not really about extravagant, flowery writing. It's not really about your ability to get your audience laughing or crying alongside you. Engaging people's emotions is not about escalating flamboyance. If you are a contractor who needs to acquire a new piece of excavation equipment, seeing an image of a father sitting at a control panel with his son on his lap may tweak your heart, but it does not answer the appropriate emotional needs your position requires of you. And every single contractor who purchases an excavator, rationalize though he or she might to support the decision, will ultimately base that decision on emotional factors.

Studies have demonstrated that when a person can't connect emotionally with whatever task he is undertaking, he will not be able to make a decision.[10] Take scheduling a doctor's appointment. You'll only schedule that appointment when it feels right, when you know the value of getting a checkup, when you have been able to imagine the benefits you will enjoy, when you can actually see yourself doing it, or when you are afraid that not doing it would be worse. You put yourself in the picture and weigh the emotional options.

Benefits versus features

When you appeal to emotions, you help your customers make their decisions. The easiest path to making an emotional connection is by focusing on the benefits—not the features—of your product or service. *Benefits are based on people; features are based on things.*

Certainly features imply benefits. But if you only list features—if you don't spell out their associated benefits for your customers—then you are hoping they'll take the time to translate each of your specified features. Few among your audience will take the time to do that for themselves.

Lisa goes to buy a musical instrument tuner to help her rehearse and practice. She examines the packaging for a Korg Orchestral Tuner. It lists six features, one of which is "built-in microphone." She can go to a number of Web sites that offer the same product and include this feature as a part of the product description. None of the Web sites explain the benefit of this feature. If Lisa's extremely intuitive, she can probably figure out its value for herself. But suppose she isn't that intuitive and doesn't like doing the research.

A built-in microphone is not a benefit, unless you know why it is important. But it sure is beneficial to have one, because that means the tuner can hear your instrument. You don't have to question if you're playing at the right pitch; the tuner can show you. You haven't got to mess with long cords that always get tangled and a separate microphone that you have to carry around and plug in. A built-in microphone makes you very portable. It's a pick-up-and-go sort of thing.

This begins to identify some of the benefits of a tuner with a built-in microphone: Lisa can easily take it anywhere; it's much easier to figure out how to use it; it streamlines her equipment needs; it can tell her if her instrument is in tune (so she hasn't got to guess if she happens to hear things a bit on the sharp or flat side).

If there's a feature, there's a benefit. And when you identify benefits, you can begin to make relevant appeals to emotions. Persona design offers you a systematic framework for helping you interpret, through empathy, what the features of your product or service will mean in terms of benefits to the different segments of your audience.

The big picture

In one hand we have the tiny detail of how we can best connect with a customer's emotional need. In the other, we have a universe of buyers, from a variety of demographic backgrounds, with constellations of psychographic attributes, that operates within the confines of a business's topology. Personas are the interface; they allow you to express the particular within the general.

We chafe when we hear sentiments, such as Kevin Roberts's, that suggest new age marketing is nothing more than a chaos lacking formulae and best practices in which the interaction between customer and business is no place for rational, reasoned information. The successes of our clients and those other businesses that are beginning to incorporate persona design to meet the emotional needs of their customers argue otherwise.

Our new age is about media and audience fragmentation. It's about the disintegration of the mass. It's not about humans suddenly failing to need and act as humans have always needed and acted. Whatever value a concept such as "sisomo," or any other new age variant, has to offer will only be realized within a context of relevance. No relevance, and it's just *wang! wang! wang!*

CHAPTER SIXTEEN

Uncovering the Knowable

I f you bring together ideas from many different sources and disciplines to reveal a different, coherent way of looking at things, you create something that is more than the sum of its parts, a gestalt. Persuasion Architecture—the discipline we have created for conceiving, planning, and developing the persuasive elements of persuasion entities—is such a gestalt.

Persuasion Architecture draws on the fields of psychology, neuroscience, marketing, sales, linguistics, information retrieval, creativity and graphic design, usability, heuristic analysis, persuasive copywriting and analytics that incorporate data-mining, testing, and optimization methodologies. All of these disciplines work together within the context of a relentless devotion to marketing accountability.

Persuasion Architecture is, in essence, a discipline that integrates the buying with the selling processes and marries that two-sided process to the marketing communications flow. Its focus, always, is persuading the customer to take action.

In applying the philosophy and principles of Persuasion Architecture, you:

- Create business-specific personas that reflect the demographic, psychological, and topologic dimensions of your audience
- Develop persuasion scenarios that meet the needs of your audience's buying decision processes and your sales process
- Integrate your multi-channel marketing efforts, based on the personas you have created, through persuasion entities
- Establish a structure that will allow you to test, measure, and optimize your results on a continuing basis, so you can manage intelligently

Personas are the centerpiece of Persuasion Architecture. Creating them is part of the most important work you can do in the entire process. Uncovery,[1] which we will now dig into deeply from this point through Chapter Twenty-Two, is the *sine qua non* when it comes to designing persuasive systems.

Uncovery

Can you imagine tackling the construction of an office building without a set of blueprints in hand? Can you imagine drawing up those blueprints with only a cursory understanding of all the questions you have to answer before you put a single line on paper? Of course you can't. You intuitively know this would at best limit how your structure worked and at worst doom your project to failure. What you really want is a comprehensive picture of every detail that could reinforce or undermine your success before you start dealing with the tangibles.

We operate in a world full of unknowables. So uncovery is the process of understanding what is knowable, and seeking to understand that from every possible known perspective. We repeatedly find that the knowledge a business needs so it can create meaningful solutions can almost always be found within the organization. It's simply waiting for someone to pull back the covers—to uncover it.

No two businesses are ever carbon copies of each other. In uncovery, our goal is to examine the topology, psychographics, and demographics as they pertain to the business in question. We're also looking to understand the culture of the organization itself. As we continue in our discussion of uncovery, you'll see it is a deep and complex evaluation of the stakeholders, the business model and objectives, the competitors, the customers, and the influences on those customers.

People don't usually get terribly excited when we first bring up uncovery. Perhaps it seems vague or even mystical to them. Perhaps they think it's a time-waster. Perhaps they already know it all. Perhaps they fear what they will learn. Perhaps they prefer to get right to what they think is the heart of the matter. Whatever the reason, businesses tend to gloss over these planning dimensions.

We cannot overemphasize the importance of uncovery. It is the foundation for every step of Persuasion Architecture. Without uncovery, not only do you lack a useful set of blueprints, you operate blind. Uncovery sets the course for everything else you do. Start by sending your project in the wrong direction, and it will be nearly impossible to steer it back on course again.

The difference between an adequate and a great uncovery lies in the level of commitment and involvement on the part of the executive decision-makers. In uncovery, we deal with all levels of business strategy, and it is entirely possible that in the reexamination of these issues, companies may need to rethink high-level decisions.

Even individuals relatively unskilled in the art of business strategy can follow our process of uncovery and achieve better-than-average results. The process is obviously more effective when performed by people with an integrative understanding of all the issues involved.

It is virtually impossible for any business to achieve comprehensive self-disclosure on its own—as we say, you can't read the label from inside the bottle. When it comes to issues in which we have a huge personal investment—our children, our homes, and our businesses—we risk losing our objectivity. It's then we risk pushing our own interests at the expense of our customers' interests.

Corporate cultures also have a way of justifying and codifying their own status quos. An uncovery that incorporates an outside perspective, balanced by the knowledge that decision-makers have of the whats and whys of their business, is far superior to one done entirely in-house. Having an informed and sensitive individual available to challenge your assumptions, in a way that only someone outside your business can, helps you achieve better results.

CHAPTER SEVENTEEN

Disclosing the Necessary

What we can know about a business does not depend only on what the business is prepared to disclose. It's important to accept that customers today can get information about products from all sorts of sources. Businesses no longer control what the customer does or does not know.

Many businesses understandably feel uncomfortable—painfully naked and vulnerable—operating in an environment where the customers are in control and demanding transparency. The days are over when a company could create a product or service and spin out the associated marketing collateral, telling customers what the company felt it was important for them to know.

In 2002, a study by J.D. Power and Associates indicated that for every one hundred new-vehicle buyers, sixty turned to the Internet for product research. They visited an average of seven Web sites in the course of their research and began the process almost two months before they actually made a purchase. Eighty-eight percent of those sixty went online *before* they visited a dealership. Eighty-two percent of those sixty visited third-party automotive Web sites, which constituted the most popular Web sites among new-vehicle buyers in the United States. Seventy-six percent of those sixty visited a manufacturer's Web site while 48 percent visited a dealer Web site. Nevertheless, only 4 percent of new-vehicle buyers in America purchased a vehicle online.[1]

While customers are interested in what manufacturers have to say about their own products, they often place greater value on what independent third parties have to say. And they increasingly pay attention to what opinionated and admittedly self-interested customers have to say through trivial and not-so-trivial gossip.

Certainly the marketing collateral for automotive purchases exists in brochures and on Web sites. But manufacturers count on salespeople to provide the critical information a customer needs, and that's a big problem in the automotive self-disclosure model: Lots of people do not want to talk to a salesperson first. And they no longer have to.

When it comes to cars, customers have an idea of which cars interest them—a result of the "push" marketing efforts of branding work.[2] But with their finely-tuned BS meters turned on, customers are aware the frontal view of marketing and the "truth" aren't necessarily the same. So they turn to online resources to "pull" the information that businesses avoid disclosing to them. And whether businesses like it or not, customers must have this information to develop the necessary confidence to complete this complex purchase.

Businesses are justifiably upset that information freely available and beyond their control has the potential to undermine brands. In November 2005, *Forbes'* cover article, "Attack of the blogs," focused on the unsupportable libelous and slanderous criminal activities some blogs engage in; it also sowed more generalized seeds of discontent and fear: blogs kill brands; negative consumer-generated-media, even if it happens to be true, is the enemy; it's "us" versus "them," and it's a battlefield in which "we" are at an unfair disadvantage.[3]

While we do not condone criminal activity, information is freely available—not hidden, not unknowable, but out in the open. Scenarios that model the customer's car-buying process without taking into account all the information that is available to that customer are simply bad scenarios. Cars don't exist in a vacuum; they have information wrapped around them that can be seen from many different angles.

Marketers today turn to market research, surveys, studies, and focus groups to ferret out information, yet when the market itself generates candid commentary, marketers perceive that as adversarial. Not so long ago, they would have said this candid information was exactly what they wanted. To embrace the level of transparency our experience economy demands, you need to come to terms with a few potentially uncomfortable truths:

- How you view yourself (as a company) is not necessarily how others view you
- The information you currently provide is not necessarily the information your customers need to develop the confidence to buy
- Efforts to keep your multi-channel efforts discreet are not likely to give positive reinforcement to your customers' experiences of your brand

When you persist in believing in these things, you risk revealing what our colleague Tamara Adlin calls "your corporate underpants." Need we say, even with a wink, this is not the sort of information your customers are clamoring for?

The Johari Window: a model for self-disclosure

What we need to achieve is a complete understanding of the modes in which people, within the context of your business, make their buying decisions and the angles from which it is possible for them to interact with you. This requires a substantial degree of self-disclosure on your part. In part, uncovery rediscovers what you know about your own business and articulate to your prospects. More importantly, it *uncovers* the critical information you know about your business and need to articulate to your prospects to influence their perception of your value to them.

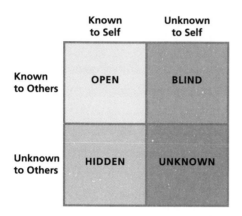

One of the best models for framing the process of self-disclosure and understanding what uncovery is meant to accomplish is the **Johari Window,** a communications model developed by Joseph Luft and Harry Ingham in the 1960s. It describes the dynamic of human interaction in terms of knowledge relationships—what is known, or not known, and to whom. And what is marketing if not self-disclosure about our key benefits?

The relationships are quite simple. There is what is known and unknown to the self (for our purposes, the business), and there is what is known and unknown to others (the customers). A four-paned "window" divides the combinations of these levels of awareness into four types: open, unknown, blind, and hidden. As mutual familiarity increases, the lines dividing the four panes move to reflect the changes in the relationship.

Open. The open quadrant represents information you and your customers know about each other. Early in the relationship, the size of this quadrant is small—there has been little time to exchange information. As you and your customers become more familiar with each other, the dividing line moves down or to the right, placing more information into the open window.

Unknown. The unknown quadrant represents information that neither party knows about the other. While it is not impossible to discover something neither the business nor its customers know about the relationship, it is very unlikely. Pursuing this area is rarely a productive effort.

Blind. The blind quadrant represents information you do not know about yourself, but your customers do know. A necessary part of uncovery is to identify what the customer knows so it can be revealed to the business.

Hidden. The hidden quadrant represents information you know about yourself but your customers do not know. Uncovering this hidden information so we can move it into the open quadrant is very often the key to a great uncovery.

We all know that organizations develop personalities. In our practice, our Persuasion Architects try to determine an organization's Myers-Briggs Type preferences (see Chapter Twenty). These preferences predispose organizations to place particular information in different quadrants of the Johari Window. This is useful—if you know where to dig you are more likely to strike a rich vein of information.

Not all information in the open quadrant is necessarily information we are happy to acknowledge. Let's suppose we are automobile manufacturers. A review in *Car and Driver* that lambastes our latest production model doesn't fill our hearts with joy, but it is still open information we have to address.

And these days, the blind quadrant really shouldn't be so blind. If there are customer concerns out there, they are possible to uncover. Awareness and understanding of how customers are talking about you—from their interests to their concerns to the very language they use to express themselves—present you with chances to develop specific, important content that addresses these issues. Even negative information gives you a potent opportunity to develop good will and better meet the needs of your customers by having the courage to address it rather than running from it.

A colleague of ours at Bazaarvoice, a managed software solution that allows online retailers to encourage and monitor customer-to-customer conversations, shared this story about how one of their clients plans to benefit from customer reviews.

An important goal for this client is to take action on negative reviews to create goodwill with vocal and influential customers. For example, the client reached out to a customer who wrote a high quality, detailed review of an item, in which he praised the item's design and features but criticized its workmanship and durability. Because the product is a bestseller with a very low failure rate, the client responded by replacing the product and asking to learn more about how the customer used the product. The net result was a very satisfied customer who will likely influence many other customers in a positive way.

Relying on the customer base to drive merchandising and marketing decisions, this same client is also using customer reviews to identify which items to promote and how to promote them. One product received eleven five-out-of-five ratings, so the client plans to feature this item with marketing copy that emphasizes the "unanimous customer approval" of the product. The company is also planning to use reviews to identify product issues and then engage vendors in research and development discussions.

Hidden truths

Information uncovered in open and blind quadrants, however, is usually not the ultimate source of trouble for any business. The biggest difficulties lie in the hidden quadrant—the information a business chooses not to disclose.

Let's go back to imagining ourselves as car manufacturers. When our latest automotive production model was built, we had teams of engineers; we spent hundreds of millions of dollars bringing this car to life. We have the answers to virtually any question a customer might ask of us, from the most common to the most arcane. We know that the design of a car is a delicate and complex intermingling of compromises. Many of the customers in our audience know this too. While we might reasonably agree the Pareto Principle (also known as the 80-20 Rule) needs to apply when it comes to how exhaustive we should be in sharing information, it's foreseeable that a customer might want to understand why we designed this engine with this particular torque, horsepower, or number of cylinders.

We have our reasons for making our automotive-design decisions. The answers we provide may not be the answers the customer was hoping for, but they represent the truth. And ultimately, if a customer consciously makes a choice in a trade-off situation—say between maneuverability and comfort—that customer is far more likely not only to be satisfied, but even delighted by the truth.

The frontal view is the marketing collateral a company creates to describe and promote its product or service. It's the best possible presentation in the best possible light. And every product and service should continue to enjoy a frontal view.

Nevertheless, either the manufacturer discloses critical information to customers, or someone else will. Doesn't it build greater confidence in a customer when the company, rather than a stranger, supplies that information? Taking responsibility for presenting all the information allows you to interact with your customers in a much larger open quadrant—you are being open about the fact this information is out there. You can provide the perspective that works in your favor and competes favorably with the angles others devise.

Take Philip Morris. They make cigarettes. You'd have to be an utter hermit not to know smoking is bad for your health, and Philip Morris would have to be the worst sort of ostrich if it remained blithely inattentive to public opinion and completely shirked its responsibility to acknowledge the risks. A visit to philipmorrisusa.com offers an interesting example of how one company provides information that doesn't meet anyone's idea of a conventional frontal view. In fact, amid prominent options to learn about smoking and health, parent resources, and how to quit smoking, the Philip Morris home page proclaims itself anti-marketing.

Digging into the Web site, you will find:

Philip Morris USA agrees with the overwhelming medical and scientific consensus that cigarette smoking causes lung cancer, heart disease, emphysema and other serious diseases in smokers. Smokers are far more likely to develop serious diseases, like lung cancer, than non-smokers. There is no safe cigarette.

To reduce the health effects of smoking, the best thing to do is to quit; public health authorities do not endorse either smoking fewer cigarettes or switching to lower-yield brands as a satisfactory way of reducing risk.

QuitAssist is a free information resource offered by Philip Morris USA. QuitAssist connects smokers who have decided to quit to a

wealth of expert quitting information from public health authorities and others.

Needless to say, Philip Morris still plans on selling cigarettes, ideally to
customers who, having made an informed, conscious choice to play
Russian roulette with their health, have no retaliatory legal leg to stand on.
Obviously, cigarette companies didn't do this voluntarily, but they tell you
"What we sell is bad for you," and they continue to make large profits.

One more car scenario

Lisa desperately needed a new car. She loves the feel of a sports car; in
fact, after the "personality" factor of a car, the feel of the drive is the most
important thing to her. But she was also constrained by practicalities—she
needed enough room to carry suitcases, groceries, instruments, sound
equipment, and even her six-foot-tall son, Zachary. A conventional sports
car was out. She was drawn to BMW's MINI Cooper, but given that she
doesn't replace her car every three years and currently lives the life of a
single parent, she wanted to be sure it was going to be the right car for her.

So Lisa began researching. She went to third-party Web sites. She read
endless customer reviews. She reviewed dealer customer-service support.
She even endured the manufacturer's Web site so she could learn something about car specs and all the options packages, determined that no
salesperson would talk down to her simply because she is a woman.

Lisa then compared the MINI to other cars she would have considered
buying. And only when she thought she had all her ducks in a row did she
go to a MINI dealer for a chat and a test drive.

Based on months of research and that test drive, Lisa became the
insanely happy owner that day of a 2004 MINI Cooper S (black body,
white roof, no stripes). These are her words:

> MINI's all over the fact they've got a great handling car that oozes
> style and is fairly safe, in as much as a car this tiny can be safe. And
> I tell people I love the way it drives. I do. But there are a lot of
> things the dealers and manufacturer don't tell you about the

MINI. Like, the gas mileage, at least for a US model, isn't what you might hope for. And the interior quality is a little on the chintzy side, even with the sport seats. And if you don't buy rear mud flaps, you'll wind up wearing the road all over the back of your car. And there's something about the aerodynamic shape that makes your windscreen a magnet for nasty flying pebbles that can leave chips. Customers mention these things if you look online.

The biggest issue—and it's really obvious if you understand the handling/suspension trade-off—is that a MINI can give you one heck of a jostling. It handles like a sports car, which means it rides like a sports car. Urban roads just aren't maintained with sports cars in mind, so while you can park almost anywhere, your teeth get a major rattling. Another MINI owner and I had a good laugh when she said BMW should throw in a complimentary sports bra for their well-endowed female customers. For a lot of people, that would be really important to know, but MINI doesn't clue you in. And MINI dealerships are often in the nice parts of town where the roads you'll test drive on are reasonably well-paved.

MINI isn't your run-of-the-mill choice for a car, and for some people, it is absolutely not the car they should be encouraged to buy. They simply won't be happy with it. I went into it with my eyes wide open. I knew the limitations. In the same breath I'm telling people how much I love my MINI, I'm also telling them the drawbacks.

If BMW were more straightforward in describing the MINI, they might have avoided the negative comments associated with it. BMW may or may not have lost a small number of sales short-term, but long-term, they would have gained even more brand evangelists.

CHAPTER EIGHTEEN

Mapping Business Topology

W eb inventor Sir Tim Berners-Lee wrote, "The world can be seen as only connections, nothing else. We think of a dictionary as the repository of meaning, but it defines words only in terms of other words . . . a piece of information is really defined only by what it's related to, and how it's related. There really is little else to meaning. The structure is everything."[1]

In both mathematics and communication networks, topology refers to the ways in which things are connected, an interpretation that can incorporate the scope of the universe and the entirety of human thought. Some believe no concept can exist in isolation, and that only the *connections* between things constitute reality. Topology—with its Greek roots meaning "knowledge of place"—is the study of the landscape of connections.

Delving into business topology requires combining art and science. This isn't the place for an exhaustive discussion of every conceivable business model or competitive landscape that has existed or could exist.

Economists and business people have studied this extensively. But let's take a moment to look at business topology in a general way.

The value of comparison

Studying business topology allows us to understand the nature of a business by comparing it to other known businesses. Sometimes these comparisons lead us to question prevailing practice; other times they provide interesting solutions we might not have considered before.

For instance, a theater and an airline share a topological element: once the doors close, any unoccupied seat remains empty and unpaid for. That is not to say theaters and airlines are in the same business, but it does show how topological similarities are not always confined to the same business category.

Likewise, sellers of produce and sellers of fashion share a similar topology in that their products have a perishable nature—although they aren't perishable in the same way. You may still manage to sell produce that is starting to wilt to someone who will eat it, but once it has spoiled, it is only suitable for sale as compost. In the fashion world, "perishability" allows for the chance that at some price, in some place, somebody might yet buy our yellow polka-dot tuxedo that was the rage last spring. These aren't the exact same thing, but the problems are similar.

Even identical topologies within the same business category may not solve their problems in the same fashion. Let's revisit the empty theater seats. Broadway theaters are not in the habit of discounting seats after the performance starts, but many London theaters are happy to do this. (We don't have enough data to know which the better approach is, but certainly both are valid approaches to resolving the same business issue.)

A classic example of the value of studying business topology is Henry Ford, whose brilliance was in understanding two elements. First, a mass market has the potential to sell larger quantities at lower costs than a customized market. Ford also recognized that automobile manufacturing was labor-intensive, which made an automobile cost-prohibitive for the workingman. His goal was to make an automobile the workingman could afford to buy.

Recognizing that labor-intensive processes were not exclusive to automobile manufacture, Ford took his inspiration from the meatpacking plants of Chicago. Instead of assembling a product, the meatpackers had devised remarkably efficient lines for disassembling carcasses of beef. They broke the entire reduction process into discrete steps, and laborers were assigned responsibility for one task. Specialization of tasks reduced the need for comprehensive training and increased the efficiency of production.

In perfecting the automotive assembly line, Ford was able to produce a Model T in ninety-three minutes. Not only could he sell it at a price a workingman could afford, he could sell it at a price a Ford employee could afford! (Of course, in utilizing this application of business topology, Henry Ford planted the seeds for the current high-cost labor structures of the modern US automobile industry, but that's another story!)

Business "flavors"

In *Good to Great: Why Some Companies Make the Leap . . . and Others Don't*, Jim Collins observes that successful businesses come in three basic flavors. A business can be operationally excellent and/or price competitive and/or customer intimate. Because of the contradictory nature of these qualities, a business may well embrace two of these qualities, but it can rarely be all three at once. [2]

Disturbed by this observation, our colleague and partner Roy H. Williams offers a fourth type of business, which he calls "path dominance." A path-dominant business simply has a better distribution model—a good example is the concession stand in a ballpark or movie theater. Such an operation is able to sell refreshments at prices that in any other context would be considered wildly overpriced, but they succeed because they enjoy a captive audience.

This "path dominance"—we could also call it "channel dominance"—is something that works to the advantage of companies like Anheuser Busch and McDonald's. Budweiser and Big Macs may not always be a customer's first choice when thinking about which beer to drink or where to grab a bite on the road. But Budweiser and Big Macs are everywhere, and many people often choose them as the default, known (and hence "safe") option.

Interestingly, Anheuser Busch, recognizing the various levels of opportunity within its business category, has recently adopted a secondary strategy of what they call "selling small":

> At Anheuser-Busch, which sells roughly half of all the beer in the United States, executives acknowledge they need to do a better job of making a "personal connection" with the customer. "It's no longer good enough to be a mass-media brand," said Bob Lachky, executive vice president of global industry development for Anheuser-Busch. "We have to learn how to sell small."[3]

Persuasion Architecture offers an exceptional framework for selling small. It allows marketers to add a level of customer intimacy ("personalization") to almost every business model. When you provide customers with relevant information, regardless of the angle from which they approach your business, you promote the feeling of intimacy with the brand.

The role of competition

Another important element in understanding the nature of a business's topology is examining the competitive landscape. Not all of a business's competitors necessarily compete for the same customers. You may sell widgets, and we may sell widgets, but if you wholesale and we retail, our competitive overlap may be minimal. Conversely, home sellers compete not only with other home sellers, but also with home remodelers. And sometimes the competition constitutes an alternative we didn't consider, which could include the customer's option to do nothing at all.

More subtle variations are possible—you might be a competitor in one aspect, yet not in others. For example, General Electric is a huge conglomerate and as such, competes with many companies. General Electric competes with financial institutions in lending. It competes with manufacturers like Westinghouse in building nuclear plants. But if General Electric were to evaluate its competitive landscape, they would find it more meaningful to look at competition by business segment rather than by competitors to the conglomerate itself.

In many respects, topological aspects of competition are better defined by viewing them through the eyes of the customer, from the bottom up rather than from the top down.

The value of topology to Persuasion Architecture

The exploration of business topology during the uncovery phase can be a virtual Pandora's box. But at the simplest level, examining the topology of your business helps you understand the structures and challenges that are present in your business category. This helps you identify the levels of familiarity and confusion potential customers can bring to their interaction with you. A manufacturer of pencils shares topological qualities with a manufacturer of computers, but an individual going about restocking her supply shelves with pencils and an individual upgrading employee desktops will approach the assumptions and questions associated with their tasks differently.

For our purposes, topology has greatest relevance to the extent it allows us to see a company from the perspective of the customer. We ultimately want to understand the functions of a business in terms of what it is able to provide its customers. So we often start thinking about topology at a deceptively simple level—it helps us maintain a customer-centric focus.

Understanding *what* you want to accomplish provides a critical framework for *how* you will go about accomplishing it. If all businesses had a C-level executive such as a Chief Persuasion Officer, that person's responsibilities would include creating a strategy for all the personas/business segments within and across all the business's persuasion entities. A big part of that responsibility would rely upon an ongoing examination of that business's landscape of connections.

CHAPTER NINETEEN

The Topology of a Sale

S ales situations readily lend themselves to topological discussions and categorization. Sales are often described using the words *business-to-consumer, business-to-business, simple sales, complex sales, peer-to-peer sales,* and many other variations. To our way of thinking, though, none of these labels really describes what is important about the sale.

As we were growing our business, we tried responding to these predefined categories of sales. Many of our readers and clients presented us with questions like these: "You use lots of retail examples, but you almost never talk about what I'm interested in, which is business-to-business. What should I be doing differently?" We often couched our language in terms of "considered sales," but, of course, this suggests there are unconsidered sales. Yet even a customer's most impulsive purchase incorporates a buying decision process that involves some level of consideration.

Ever try to get a handle on what *exactly* constitutes a considered purchase or complex sale? We have. We've searched on the various sales topology terms and discovered the following: A considered purchase or complex sale has to do with the things you might find listed in comparative consumer reports. It includes stuff like travel, electronics, furniture, and high-end cookware. A considered purchase costs more money, has less market competition, and is a more unique product. Our problem with all this? Vagueness in a definition is definitely not a helpful quality!

We also discovered a wilderness of fuzzy thinking about the nature of business-to-consumer versus business-to-business:

> One thing differentiating business-to-business marketing from consumer marketing is a product's price tag. B-to-b purchases, like machine tools or enterprise software, usually start in the six-figure range. This is why the average b-to-b sale involves seven decision-makers . . . [and] why b-to-b marketers call them "considered purchases." Consumer goods are a bit cheaper and less risky to buy.[1]

> In business-to-business, most transactions are a considered purchase. Example: no one runs out and buys thirteen jet engines on a lark. There are no frequent buyer programs for $250,000 machine tools or $500,000 enterprise software solutions. A mentor distinguished consumer purchases from business-to-business purchases like this: "Buying the wrong toothpaste leaves a bad taste in your mouth. Making the wrong business-to-business purchase can cost you your job." And that's just one reason why these sales are complex.[2]

How much time do you really want to spend debating or trying to define the classification of your sales process? Whatever label you decide on, it's not going to bring you an inch closer to being able to design a more effective persuasive system. Our advice is to forego the conventional sales topologies. Think in terms of your persuasive process. Whether a decision needs to be made by a committee, a couple, or a solitary person, we still need to persuade one individual at a time. And the cognitive models for the sale of a pack of gum have much in common with the sale of commercial aircraft engines—as we discuss below, the process simply involves a greater degree of complexity.

Recall the three questions we discussed in Chapter Eight, which define every element within any persuasive system:

1. What is the action we want someone to take?

2. Who are we trying to persuade to take the action?

3. What does that person need in order to feel confident taking that action?

When your efforts are focused on answering these questions, it doesn't matter whether you are working business-to-business or business-to-consumer. Defining the topology of any sales situation is much better understood in terms of its complexity.

The four dimensions of sales complexity

We have developed our own model for a meaningful understanding of sales topology. When we examine a business's sales process, we evaluate it in terms of need, risk, knowledge, and consensus.

You'll notice these dimensions suggest sales topology is focused on the customer's perceptions and experiences, not the role the business occupies in relation to the customer. And that's exactly how we feel any discussion of sales topology in the context of designing persuasive systems should be framed.

Not a single one of these factors is shockingly new; marketers have always been sensitive to them. It's just that people have never had a systematic way to work with them.

Need. We can describe need on a continuum that ranges from critical to necessary to luxury. Through uncovery, we want to understand how urgent the felt need for the product or service is. How quickly are customers likely to make their decisions to buy? Will the need be satisfied by a one-time purchase (either impulsive or momentous), or is the need ongoing? Customers might be willing to compromise their thoroughness for a casual one-time deal, but if that one-time deal is something like a house or if they are choosing a long-term business relationship to satisfy an ongoing need, things get significantly more complicated.

Risk. Risk can be perceived as pertaining to the physical body, a career, self-esteem, or self-actualization. In essence, the dimension of risk echoes the levels of human needs described in Maslow's hierarchy (see Chapter Two). We want to understand how financially risky the sale is. While price may not be an ultimate decision factor in a purchase (in many cases, safety and trust trump price), increasing financial risk requires a more intricate persuasive structure. Risk may also be associated with compromises to health, as when individuals or medical professionals have to make treatment choices. Or even, for that matter, when someone simply evaluates the safety of an herbal remedy.

Knowledge. Knowledge contains depth and breadth, which can widen and deepen. Changes in knowledge can redefine the perception of need or risk, and often, acquiring knowledge can lead you to realize you know considerably less than you thought you did. Uncovery helps reveal how difficult it is for customers to understand the nature of the product or service, or the procedures for buying. What do they need to know? A persuasive process must eliminate the friction of confusion or ignorance. Knowledge dimensions for the buying decision can differ based on who is doing the buying: Is the customer buying for herself (she will be the end user), or is she buying on behalf of another (as in the case of a purchasing agent)? The knowledge assumptions and language—especially jargon— that work for one may be totally inappropriate for the other.

Consensus. We can understand consensus issues as decisions that are made anonymously, personally, or by groups. It's important to understand how many people you have to persuade and at which point in the process you have to persuade them. An individual? An individual and her significant other? Several end-users and heads-of-department? *Consensus is the dimension most people fail to define well when they design persuasive systems.*

Bryan makes an *anonymous* decision when he picks up a candy bar at the airport and eats it. No one else influenced Bryan's choice. Consensus is not always about how many people will actually make the decision; it's also about how many people will influence the decision.

Bryan goes online and buys a shirt. It arrives; he carefully unpacks it and puts it away in anticipation of its debut. The morning he decides to wear it, he irons it so it looks crisp and fresh. As he's getting ready to leave the house, his wife comes to kiss him good-bye. Half inviting a compliment, Bryan looks in the mirror and says, "Here's my new shirt." His wife knows he's fishing for a compliment, but in the instant her face betrays a fleeting expression of horror, Bryan knows he'll never wear that shirt again. That fleeting look influences his *personal* shirt-buying decisions.

A *group* decision is required when Bryan, the partners, the accountant, and the attorney must agree on a business investment. Each individual within the group will have his or her own way of interpreting the dimensions of need, risk, and knowledge as they pertain to the decision, and the persuasive system will have to acknowledge those needs as well.

The nature of the sale

Need, risk, knowledge, and consensus will apply differently depending on the nature of your sale. For example, home computers aren't a terribly high-risk product anymore, but many people still don't understand the technology. They'll take their time acquiring information before deciding to buy one. However, Lisa can tell you it's a completely different story if the one and only computer upon which an Internet writer depends just crashed and needs to be replaced immediately.

By the same token, you might take a while to consider the purchase of a furnace if you are building a new house, but if your existing furnace breaks on a blisteringly cold winter day, you need to replace it immediately.

Almost no one would say that buying a pencil is a complex process. Knowledge of pencils isn't generally a problem, and having the wrong one isn't very risky. Nevertheless, for a large company, the purchase of a case of pencils or a single pencil from a new vendor might require a more formal process involving several individuals or departments to sign off on a purchase order. Because consensus is necessary, you now have a more complex pencil sale.

These factors can also be interdependent. The more you know about something, the more you may perceive the risks involved. Conversely, more knowledge may afford you the perception of less risk.

The individual facing heart surgery will consider the relationship between knowledge and risk differently than will the heart surgeon. As will the individual investor staking his life earnings on options, compared to the options trader for whom these transactions are daily occurrences. In similar manner, changes in the perception of risk may incline you to reevaluate your level of need. If that heart surgeon explains the risks of a procedure far outweigh the potential benefits, you may decide the operation you thought you desperately needed isn't nearly so necessary.

Because the resulting information will be critical to persona and scenario design, uncovery examines and analyzes these dimensions in detail. We use a scale from 1 (low) to 5 (high) to help us plot dimensions of complexity on a visual representation we call a Complexogram. We'll be the first to tell you this is a subjective process. But it offers us a reference and direction that we continue to investigate as we dig deeper into our understanding of the business and designing personas.

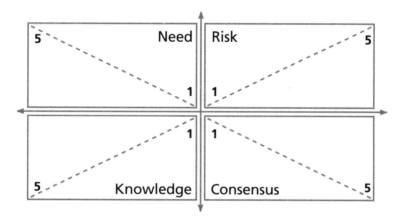

Four types of buyers

Whatever sort of traffic you get—store, Web site, catalog—a potential customer has crossed your path. There are four different kinds of customers.

Accidentals. Some find you accidentally and are not in the market for your goods or services, certainly not now and maybe not ever. We think, for purposes of our discussion at least, you can ignore these people. However, if you have more of them than you think you should, it may be time to reexamine things. On the one hand, you may just be in a highly trafficked location where lots of unqualified people are wandering in. This can't be helped. On the other hand, you may be targeting a pay-per-click advertisement with a keyword that is too broad—for instance, "boats" when what you sell are model boats.

Knows Exactly. These people know exactly what they want, down to the model number (or its equivalent). We'd also include in this category those who might not be able to pinpoint a unique identifier but can describe exactly what they need.

Knows Approximately. Next are the people who know approximately what they want. They are in the market to buy, but they have not made their final decision on exactly what they want to buy. For example, they know they need to replace their hanging-on-by-a-thread athletic shoes, but they haven't narrowed their choice down to a particular brand or model.

Just Browsing. And then there are those people who are in "browsing" mode. They're window shoppers who aren't necessarily planning to take any specific action. In many ways, these individuals can be difficult to distinguish from the previous two categories of potential customers— these are people who, when they run across just the right thing, will take action. This might be the sort of person who knew that within the next year he wanted to upgrade his digital camera.

Or it might be someone like Lisa, who loves teapots. She has many of them. But she's always looking at teapots, and when she discovers a business that carries them, she's quite content to browse the selection to see if there's anything of interest. Even though she doesn't actually *need* another teapot, she might well buy one.

It's important to understand that these categories of potential customers essentially reflect stages of the buying decision process. But having described these categories, it's equally important to understand that none of these people are any more likely to take action than another. The person who knows exactly what he wants can be easily distracted by other offers, whereas the person who is simply browsing can become an immediate buyer. The differentiations describe where people can be within their own minds or within the buying cycle.

This is the simplest way of describing the universe of buyers. We'll develop this further in our discussion of psychographics, where we explain how psychographic preferences affect this universe of buyers.

Relational and transactional customers

At Wizard Academy, our partner, Roy Williams, teaches that every person has a transactional and relational mode of shopping:

1. **Transactional shoppers** are focused only on today's transaction and give little thought to the possibility of future purchases.

2. Their only fear is of paying more than they had to pay. Transactional shoppers are looking for price and value.

3. They enjoy the process of comparing and negotiating and will likely shop at several stores before making their decision to purchase.

4. Transactional shoppers do their own research so they won't need the help of an expert. Consumer Reports are published primarily for the transactional shopper.

5. Because they enjoy the process, transactional shoppers don't consider their time spent shopping to be part of the purchase price.

6. Anxious to share the "good deal" they've found, transactional shoppers are excellent sources of word-of-mouth advertising.

1. **Relational shoppers** consider today's transaction to be one in a long series of many future purchases. They are looking less for a product than for a store in which to buy it.

2. Their only fear is of making a poor choice. Relational shoppers will purchase as soon as they have confidence. Will your store and your staff give them this confidence they seek?

3. They don't enjoy the process of shopping and negotiating.

4. Relational shoppers are looking principally for an expert they can trust.

5. They consider their time to be part of the purchase price.

6. Confident that they have found "the right place to buy," relational shoppers are very likely to become repeat customers.[3]

Each of us can be transactional *and* relational shoppers; we can be transactional in some product or service areas and relational in others. Understanding the difference between transactional and relational needs allows you to create language and scenarios that address these buying modes among your personas.

Is *everyone* your customer?

When we ask our clients this question, everybody's immediate response is, "Yeah, sure!" But as we get into creating personas and start looking at how people buy your goods or services, we'll discover that your business may not be configured in such a way as to please every potential customer.

On top of which, not everyone is going to be your customer. In fact, there are probably some you specifically do not want. Keep this in mind: you're not a $100 bill; not everyone is going to like you.

CHAPTER TWENTY

The Human Operating System

S ince the great Greek thinkers, people have observed that human personalities, while as unique as thumbprints, do exhibit dramatic
commonalities. Our consulting psychologist, Dr. Richard "Nick"
Grant, Jr., was the first to refer to these commonalities as the "human
operating system." Much of the information in this chapter is based on
what Dr. Grant teaches at Wizard Academy.

Many of the great philosophers who have dabbled in theories about
personality have identified four dominant temperaments. In 370 BC,
Hippocrates identified them as Sanguine, Choleric, Phlegmatic, and
Melancholic. Carl Jung (1875–1961) called them Feeler, Thinker, Sensor,
and Intuitor. More recently, David Keirsey identified Idealists, Rationals,
Guardians, and Artisans.

Observations about temperament and type preferences are now
understood as a function of brain lateralization, or how the brain uses its
separate but connected right and left hemispheres. Both sides of our
brains are different, just as our body is asymmetrical—our right and left

sides are not mirror images of each other. These asymmetrical design limitations of brain and body create the dynamic of the human operating system. Our "limitations" define what's possible. For all of us, our abilities and preferences lie between the extreme of the right and the extreme of the left.

The most familiar brain lateralization exercise is right- versus left-handedness. Left-handed people are right-brain dominant, while right-handed people are left-brain dominant. These are, of course, preferences, not delimitations. If you pick up a pen and sign your name with your non-preferred hand, you still are able to do it. Our preference and years of practice means that one simply feels better than the other.

The same is true for personality type preferences.

Humans are amazingly complex creatures, and any classification scheme unavoidably simplifies this complexity. In addition, each person is more than one classic personality type. We are delightful mixtures—one type may predominate, but others come into play, often influenced by environmental factors, social factors, even ephemeral moods.

But the details of our complexity and uniqueness do not provide us with constructive frameworks when it comes to selling and buying. It would be a gargantuan task to design a persuasive system that met the unique needs of 6,481,394,779 individuals.[1] Even if it were technologically possible, you'd have to question whether doing it ultimately had merit. One-to-one marketing and true personalization are perhaps unattainable ideals. And that may be a good thing.

To create manageable and useful information that can benefit sales and service communication, marketing, and even product development, we must look to some commonalities.

The background for modes of buying

We base our persona work on the theory behind the Myers-Briggs Type Indicator (MBTI), developed during World War II by Katherine Briggs and her daughter Isabelle Myers to help people identify and understand their type preferences.

Their work followed from and expanded on the work Carl Jung had presented in his book *Psychological Types*. Over fifty years of research, millions of administered tests, and thousands of applied studies have contributed to establishing the test's credibility, and it is considered an authoritative psychological model. Below you will see how the MBTI describes so much of what marketers would like to know about what goes on in the minds of customers. We have also incorporated many of David Keirsey's ideas in his work on temperament.

Our discussion of these principles is greatly oversimplified here. There are books dedicated to personality.[2] It's a fascinating subject. The important thing to keep in mind is that preferences are never good or bad, right or wrong. They are simply the way we prefer to interact with the world around us.

Myers-Briggs theory identifies sixteen different "types," based on a person's preferences along four different dichotomies. The dichotomies are similar to a continuum-like scale.

The Sixteen Types			
ISTJ	ISFJ	INFJ	INTJ
ISTP	ISFP	INFP	INTP
ESTP	ESFP	ENFP	ENTP
ESTJ	ESFJ	ENFJ	ENTJ

Dichotomies	
Extroversion	Introversion
Sensing	INtuition
Thinking	Feeling
Judging	Perceiving

Extroversion-Introversion. The Extroversion-Introversion dichotomy identifies where we turn for our sources of energy. Extroverts draw energy from the outside world of people and activities, introverts from an internal world of ideas and impressions. At the end of a work day, when we all need to recharge our batteries to carry on with the evening, an extrovert might turn to conversations with others, while an introvert would often want to be alone for a while.

Within the selling process, extroversion and introversion characterize how we initiate and engage in a relationship—extroverts prefer to "talk it out," while introverts prefer to "think it through."

In our practice, we assume that when customers are online, whether they are themselves introverts or extroverts, they are utilizing a preference for introversion. Why? The Internet is a one-to-one interaction between the visitor and whichever online resource he or she is interacting with. There is no face-to-face interpersonal contact. If the visitor subsequently picks up the phone and calls a 1-800 number, he is now utilizing a preference for extroversion.

Sensing-Intuition. Sensing and Intuition is the dichotomy that identifies how we gather information and the ways in which we are aware of things, people, events, and ideas around us. This involves the kind of information we prefer to notice. Sensing individuals gather "concrete and actual" information primarily through the five senses—how they see, hear, taste, touch, and smell the world. Intuitive individuals gather information seemingly through a "sixth sense" and value emerging patterns, or what might be.

In the sales process, we use sensing and intuition preferences when we investigate needs. Sensing types look for specifics and details; intuitors favor "the big picture" and interesting connections.

Thinking-Feeling. Decision-making, or how we reach conclusions about the information we have gathered, is the basis for the Thinking-Feeling dichotomy. In essence, our stated preference here reflects whether we are more likely to go with our heads or our hearts. Thinkers organize information objectively and logically, feeling people in a subjective, value-oriented way. This does not mean thinking types don't feel or feeling types don't think, it only refers to whether individuals prefer to use thoughts or feelings to make decisions.

Thinking and feeling suggest a course of action in the sales process. Thinking types pay attention to the logical implications while feeling types are concerned about the impact on people.

Judging-Perceiving. The Judging-Perceiving dichotomy describes how we organize and structure our lives, specifically in relation to time management. Do you prefer to plan things thoroughly or do you prefer to act spontaneously? Judgment indicates a preference for living an organized life with few "loose ends." Perception indicates a preference for living a spontaneous life with many options.

Within the sales process, judging and perceiving bear strongly on obtaining agreement and closing. Judging types take pleasure in making the decision; perceiving types enjoy exploring all the possibilities and putting off the decision.

Extroversion, Sensing, Thinking, and Judging seem to be left-brain oriented modes. Introversion, Intuition, Feeling, and Perceiving appear to be right-brain oriented modes.

For any given individual, these preferences are not necessarily predictive of behavior. Native preferences are always influenced by context. We may prefer to organize our surroundings to the nth degree, but there will always be circumstances that require us to be spontaneous. Individuals whose preferences fall toward one extreme of a dichotomy very often have to learn skills that allow them to function outside their comfort zone—for example, to manage in a mostly extroverted situation, the introvert must learn to cope using the opposite preference.

For our purposes, the importance of this framework of the human operating system is not to identify individuals or their individual preferences, but to identify modes of interaction, information-gathering, and decision-making. This is where we get an idea of the angles people will prefer for approaching the information they require.

Four temperaments

Myers did not explicitly address the concepts of temperament and character in her personality work. David Keirsey, along with Marilyn Bates, less interested in "what's in the mind" and more interested in long-term behavior patterns, reintroduced temperament theory in its modern form. Keirsey later merged his temperament work with the Myers-Briggs dichotomy labels.[3]

Unlike Myers and Jung, who saw Extroversion and Introversion as the "first cut" in defining type, Keirsey sees Intuition (abstract and introspective) and Sensing (concrete and observant) as representing the first cut in terms of preference patterns in long-term behavior. He then associates Feeling and Thinking with the Intuition side, Judging and Perceiving with the Sensing side.[4]

In this manner, he identifies four primary temperaments:

1. Sensing/Judging (SJ)

2. Sensing/Perceiving (SP)

3. Intuitive/Feeling (NF)

4. Intuitive/Thinking (NT)

Temperament			
(SJ, SP, NF, NT)			
iStJ	iSfJ	iNFj	iNTj
iStP	iSfP	iNFp	iNTp
eStP	eSfP	eNFp	eNTp
eStJ	eSfJ	eNFj	enTj

Modes for Persuasion Architecture

As Persuasion Architects, our interest is in modes of preferred behavior within a specific context—buying. Since people operate within the parameters, or bounds, of their human operating system, we can reasonably assume that the set of all possible associated behaviors falls within these parameters. We've given intuitive labels that reflect the associated buying modality to Keirsey's four primary temperaments, which are reflective of behavior patterns. This way, most people readily understand what they mean.

1. Methodical (SJ)

2. Spontaneous (SP)

3. Humanistic (NF)

4. Competitive (NT)

	Logic	Emotion
Fast	Competitive (What)	Spontaneous (Why)
Slow	Methodical (How)	Humanistic (Who)

We find it is often easier for people to quickly conceptualize these four modes when we talk about them in terms of their reliance on either logic (a left-brain function) or emotion (a right-brain function) modified by the pace at which these modes tend to make decisions.

Let's examine each of these modes in more detail. We speak of these modes as if they were people, which we find often helps us identify better with them. When we present a piece of sample copy, we have identified the words someone operating in this mode would be most drawn to.

Methodical (SJ). Methodical types need to be prepared and organized to act. For them, task completion is its own reward. These individuals appreciate facts, hard data, and information presented in a logical manner as documentation of truth. They enjoy organization and completion of detailed tasks. They do not appreciate the "personal touch," and they abhor disorganization. They fear negative surprises and irresponsibility above all. Those who are Methodical have a strong internal frame of reference. They prefer to think and speak about details and specifics. They compare everything to a standard ideal and look for mismatches (what's wrong or what's missing).

Attitude:	Businesslike, detail-oriented
Using Time:	Disciplined, methodically paced
Question:	How can your solution solve this problem?
Approach:	Provide hard evidence and superior service

Sample Copy: Our approach is timed to meet your objectives. The bottom line is that your results are guaranteed. ***Explore our methodology*** to discover how thousands of clients just like you have been delighted.

Representatives: C3PO in *Star Wars,* Dr. Carrie Weaver on *ER*, Linus from *Peanuts,* Eeyore from *Winnie the Pooh,* Main Street USA in Disney's Magic Kingdom

Spontaneous (SP). Spontaneous types must live in the moment. Their sensing preference makes them most grounded in the immediate world of the senses. This, coupled with their perceiving preference, helps them to remain poised and present in any situation. They are available, flexible, and engaged in a personal quest for action and impact, which defines who they are. For the Spontaneous, integrity means the unity of impulse with action. These individuals appreciate the personalized touch and are in search of new and exciting experiences. They dislike dealing with traditional details, and are usually quick to reach a decision. They fear "missing out" on whatever life has offer.

Attitude:	Personal, activity-oriented
Using Time:	Spontaneous, fast-paced
Question:	Why is your solution best to solve the problem now?
Approach:	Address immediate needs with relevant credible options

Sample Copy: **Our approach is timed to meet your objectives.** The bottom line is that your results are guaranteed. Explore our methodology to discover how thousands of clients just like you have been delighted.

Representatives: Hans Solo in *Star Wars,* Vivian Ward in *Pretty Woman,* Snoopy in *Peanuts,* Tigger in *Winnie the Pooh,* Adventureland in Disney's Magic Kingdom

Humanistic (NF). Humanistic types have a tendency to put others' needs before their own and are often uncomfortable accepting gifts or allowing others to do anything for them. They are very creative and entertaining. They enjoy helping others and highly value the quality of relationships. They are usually slow to reach a decision. They fear separation. Those who are Humanistic are good listeners and are generally willing to lend a sympathetic ear. They focus on acceptance, freedom, and helping. They generally prefer the big picture. They greatly value human development, including their own.

Attitude:	Personal, relationship-oriented
Using Time:	Open-ended, slow-paced
Question:	Who has used your solution to solve my problem?
Approach:	Offer testimonials and incentives

Sample Copy: Our approach is timed to meet your objectives. The bottom line is that your results are guaranteed. Explore our methodology to **discover how thousands of clients just like you have been delighted.**

Representatives: Luke Skywalker in *Star Wars,* Bridget Jones in *Bridget Jones's Diary,* Charlie Brown in *Peanuts,* Pooh in *Winnie the Pooh,* Fantasyland in Disney's Magic Kingdom.

Competitive (NT). Competitive types seek competence in themselves and others. They want to understand and control life. Driven by curiosity, a Competitive is often preoccupied with learning and has a deep appreciation for challenges. They enjoy being in control, are goal-oriented, and are looking for methods for completing tasks. Once their vision is clear, they usually reach decisions quickly. They fear loss of control. Those who are Competitive are highly motivated, success- and goal-oriented, hard-working, image-conscious, good planners, and good at promoting their ideas. They are able to subordinate their present needs to develop future success. They can be intense, very persuasive about getting their own way, and are particularly irritated by inefficiency.

Attitude:	Businesslike, power-oriented
Using Time:	Disciplined, strategically paced
Question:	What can your solution do for me?
Approach:	Provide rational options, probabilities, and challenges

Sample Copy: Our approach is timed to meet your objectives. The **bottom line is that your results are guaranteed.** Explore our methodology to discover how thousands of clients just like you have been delighted.

Representatives: Yoda and Princess Lea in *Star Wars*, Lucy in *Peanuts*, Rabbit in *Winnie the Pooh*, Tomorrowland in Disney's Magic Kingdom.

The questions they ask

Different modes are likely to lead with different types of questions, which reflect their information priorities and the pace of their deliberations.

Those who are **Methodical** focus on language that answers HOW questions.

- What are the details?
- What's the fine print?
- How does this work?
- What's the process you use?
- Can you take me through this step-by-step?
- How can I plan ahead?
- What are the product specs?
- What proof do you have?
- Can you guarantee that?

Those who are **Spontaneous** focus on language that combines WHY (and sometimes WHEN) questions.

- How can you get me to what I need quickly?
- Do you offer superior service?
- Can I customize your product or service?
- Can you help me narrow down my choices?
- How quickly can I take action and achieve my goals?
- How will this let me enjoy life more?

Those who are **Humanistic** focus on language that answers WHO questions.

- How will your product or service make me feel?
- Who uses your products/service?
- Who are you? Tell me who is on your staff, and let me see bios.
- What will it feel like to work with you?
- What experience have others had with you?
- Can I trust you?
- What are your values?
- How will this help me strengthen relationships?

Those who are **Competitive** focus on language that answers WHAT questions.

- What are your competitive advantages?
- Why are you a superior choice?
- Are you a credible company?
- How can you help me be more productive?
- How can you help make me look cutting edge?
- What are your credentials?

■ What is your research?

■ How can you help me achieve my goals?

Application to business topology

Very often, the business topology has a direct impact on the modes in which customers buy, independent of how those customers might prefer to buy.

While a spontaneous individual might be involved in the purchase of accounting software, the topology of accounting software suggests we cannot spend much time focusing on the spontaneous needs. The individual may be spontaneous, but in this acquisition, he will be required to draw upon non-preferred modes within his operating system.

Application to the sales process

As we interweave the buying decision process with the sales process, we always need to pay attention to how the sales process evolves and how that will impact customer needs along the way.

When we talk about initiating and sustaining the customer relationship, we can focus on the Myers-Briggs dichotomy of extroversion and introversion, whether people prefer to talk it out or think it through. Tactics and language that an extrovert will warm to will often drive the introvert away.

In the investigating needs phase, it's important that we understand the differences between the need to feel grounded in specifics (sensing) and the need to see the big picture, uncluttered with detail (intuition). When we suggest appropriate actions, we need to consider the potential needs for logical implications (thinking) and valuing the impact on people (feeling).

When we move to closure, we need to address the ways we can help our customers feel confident about finalizing their decisions. Time frames, a firm acknowledgement of what the customer and we have agreed to, and statements dealing with what the customer can expect next appeal to the Judging preference. Those who express a preference for

Perception value examining and reviewing all their options. They need time to reflect—someone using this preference does not respond well to a pressured close.

The universe of buyers revisited

Now we have a more meaningful context for reexamining the universe of buyers that we discussed in the previous chapter.

This graphic represents a merger between the three categories of potential customers that can cross our path—those who know exactly what they want, those who know approximately what they want, and those who are just browsing—and the four buying modes we have derived from personality

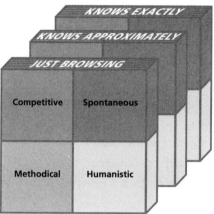

type and temperament research. In all, there are twelve possible states, and there are shades of gray in between. The art is in understanding which of these apply in your situation.

This is the basic framework that allows us to begin understanding how different modes—for example, Spontaneous or Humanistic—will interact with us depending on where they are in their buying decision processes. It's our point of departure for persona creation and scenario development.

A just-browsing customer who is operating in a Competitive modality is very different from a just-browsing customer who is operating in a Humanistic modality. They will be asking different questions, for which you will need to provide different answers in ways that will appeal to their specific needs. Ultimately, the needs you must address are the emotional needs associated with their preferences. The logic and order that appeals to the Methodical type and that the Methodical type must have to develop confidence will fail to persuade the spontaneous.

Emotion and confidence revisited

In Chapter Fifteen, we discussed the true nature of the "emotional future" that Saatchi & Saatchi CEO and "sisomo" proponent Kevin Roberts imagined. We explained that when we are unable to make the emotional connections that allow us to imagine ourselves taking action and enjoying the benefits of having taken that action, we fundamentally cannot make decisions.

Our ability to perceive and appreciate our three-dimensional realities takes place in the prefrontal cortex of the brain—the same part of the brain that is responsible for imagination and making decisions. When that area of the brain is damaged, decision-making is impaired.

Copy that emphasizes verbs and action-oriented words helps us imagine ourselves taking action. Language and processes that meet our *preference-based emotional needs* for order or bottom lines or adventure or relationships helps persuade us to take actions in reality.

The emotional needs that satisfy our preferences—whether native or the ones we must draw on to accomplish our tasks—are the qualities we need to speak to in our persuasive systems.

Why is this critical? When we have met our fundamental preference-based emotional needs, our confidence increases. And we *must* feel confidence—trust, safety, security—to act. We've mentioned that friction is the experience of cognitive dissonance, and that cognitive dissonance occurs when we lack the confidence to decide. It's one of the reasons why a product might not seem right for us one day, yet the same product on a different day or in a different store could be just the ticket.

A good persuasive system is designed to give you the confidence to move forward, to make each decision in a series of decisions that brings you closer to satisfying your goal. Even the most Methodical person, making the most Methodical buying decision, is really satisfying an emotional need that is strongly influenced by personal preference and temperament.

Choosing Personas

O K. So now you know that different customers have different buying processes based on demographics, psychographics, and topologies. Terrific. But just knowing that different customers buy in different ways isn't enough. You have to sort out those buying modalities so you can accommodate them in your persuasive system. And you have to turn those "modalities" into "personas" you can actually understand and relate to. You must feel you know these personas personally.

Demographics allow us to segment some of the *features* that will be essential to our personas. For example, the recipient of the engagement ring is much more likely to be female. Demographic data also allow us to look at parameters such as income or geographic location, so we can decide how those apply to our business topology. When buying an engagement ring, a twenty-four-year-old male with a household income of $38,000 will probably have different buying needs than a forty-two-year-old male with a household income of $245,000. A man shopping for an engagement ring may have different buying needs than a woman shopping for ideas for an engagement ring.

Psychographics allow us to segment *needs* that will be essential to our personas. A Methodical and a Competitive customer will not ask the same kinds of questions or want the same kinds of information. A Methodical customer will probably ask many more questions and want much more information than will a Competitive customer. In our diamond-buying example, a Methodical customer may need lots of technical information about diamonds, whereas a Competitive one may need to know which diamond is the most brilliant—which diamond has the highest "bling" factor.

Topology allows us to segment by *complexity of sale*. Remember—*knowledge, need, risk,* and *consensus* (see Chapter Nineteen). The nature of the concerns in these dimensions depends on your business and who is doing the buying.

When we were developing Complexograms for Leo Schachter's branded Leo Diamond Web site, we got responses that showed how different people evaluated the dimensions of need, risk, knowledge, and consensus. A young man about to buy his fianceé an engagement ring might perceive a greater financial *risk* than would an older, more financially well-off man. An ambitious, young social climber might perceive a greater *need* for a big, beautiful diamond than would a less materialistic, romantic young lady. The *consensus* dimension for a man shopping by himself for an engagement ring is on the *personal* level, whereas the consensus dimension for a couple shopping together is on the *group* level—approval comes from both parties, and possibly even outside parties including friends or family.

By combining all three—demographics, psychographics, and topology—you can then begin to understand motivation. Motivation is the crown jewel of personas—but you have to have a complete picture of a persona to truly understand his or her motivation. You can only assess motivation within the full context of a persona's life, not just his or her interaction with your particular product.

"How many personas?"

That's almost always the first question people ask us. We talk about twelve possible this and sixteen that and four these. Surely we must know, up front, exactly how many personas your persuasive system needs. Our quick and dirty answer is, "At least two." At the very least, a persuasive system has to meet needs that are either logic-based or emotion-based. In most situations, however, this is insufficient. We can only realistically answer that question when we near the end of the uncovery process. Uncovery concludes with the creation of personas.

You've probably been thinking about what we've been saying so far and trying to apply it to your business. (It's actually not a bad idea to finish reading the book before you return to this—when you can grasp the entire picture, it's easier to fit the pieces into place.) We've been posing questions about a business's core values, the buying modalities within your audience, your competition, demographics, what you measure, sales complexity, business topology, and the universe of buyers. You may have noticed that when you try to answer these questions, many of them don't have one answer, but rather have seemingly contradictory answers.

We find people often assume they need as many personas as they have market segments. The marketing team for one of our clients, a well-known market leader with a dominant share in their category, called us in to help them develop personas. They gave us an introductory presentation in which they shared their first attempt to develop personas. They were certain, based on their market segments, they needed forty-two.

We were in the delicate situation of knowing they were probably incorrect; but at that point we lacked the business data to challenge their assumptions. After several weeks of developing personas, we had brought the number down to seven, although we thought the correct number was six. In the wireframing[1] stage, the client was able to see that two of their seven personas bought identically, and finally agreed six was the necessary number. Personas are not exclusively based on market segmentation—that's just one factor we can consider.

In our experience, you can get away with as few as two personas only if you have a very simple sale. In general though, most persuasive systems we have worked with require between three and seven personas. If you come up with fewer than three or more than seven, it's possible you're on the wrong track. You may be oversimplifying something that is more complex. Or you may be trying to deal with more than one business unit (in which case, it may be advantageous to redefine the persuasive system by business units rather than the business as an entirety).

Sources of insight

The discussions that take place during uncovery, contradictory though they can seem at first, prove invaluable for identifying the issues we must address as we turn to creating personas.

Who should be involved in these discussions? Marketing, of course. But often the best uncovery insights come from sales people and customer-service people, individuals who have daily encounters with customers and understand their questions and concerns.

In addition to interviews, it's essential to go to the Web. The Web offers a vast array of information from people discussing their questions and concerns in public forums that include blogs and discussion groups. You'll gain invaluable insight into how your customers view your product and the language they use. In that language, you'll find a wealth of information, especially for the world of keyword research.

Keywords reveal intent

Keyword research, as search engine marketers typically practice it, tries to figure out which words and phrases to target for optimization so marketers can attract searchers to their Web sites. Many search engine marketers operate from a technical perspective—they want to understand the ramifications of a search engine's algorithms and play them in a way that insures their results get the highest rankings. It can get pretty cut-throat.

Unfortunately, this flavor of search engine marketer usually pays little attention to the level of intent the search query reveals. Mechanistically plugging keywords and key phrases into your Web site doesn't mean you actually address the intent behind those searches. And if you don't address intent, you haven't really benefited your Web site's persuasive system.

Keyword research is an excellent way to gather insights into the types of questions customers are asking at the precise moment they are focusing attention on the buying process. After all, what is a keyword search if not a question you're trying to answer?

Often the nature of these questions can help us define unique perspectives for our personas. For example, lots of keyword researchers would tell you the key phrases "stylish diamond" and "cheapest diamond" are contradictory. To us, there's no contradiction here. These two phrases simply suggest two different personas that a diamond business's persuasive system can easily accommodate.

The great value in keyword research lies in its ability to help you identify possible personas, develop language that reflects how your customers actually talk about and frame the problems for which they seek solutions, and identify other words that will help trigger customer response.

Finding the triggers

Developing and incorporating what we call "trigger words" into your copy and content is essential to persuading your customers. What are trigger words? They're words that "trigger" a response in your customers— they're words your customers use to describe their problems as well as the benefits and solutions they seek. Trigger words can include keywords in the traditional search engine sense. But they can also expand on the keyword.

For example, "The 4C's" may be a keyword that a person types into a search engine so she can learn more about diamonds and the four qualities for evaluating a diamond. A trigger phrase for that person might be "make an educated decision." "Make an educated decision" is not something she is likely to type into a search engine, but it is language that appeals to her. It is language that speaks to her needs and motivations. It is language that increases her confidence because it communicates that you understand and want to satisfy her needs. It is language that persuades her.

Search engine marketers may be able to deliver traffic to your door by identifying keyword queries, but your persuasive system still bears the responsibility for turning that traffic into buyers. When customers arrive, they immediately look for the words they used in their queries as evidence they are in the right place. But they also look for more. They look for language that reinforces the query *and* expands on it in a way that acknowledges the inferred buying modality. They look for trigger words.

Let's look more closely at the way keywords and trigger words work together.

David Commonsense is one of the personas we created for our client, Leo Schachter, wholesalers of the leading branded diamond, the Leo Diamond.

A Methodical persona, David wants lots of specific information. Keywords and phrases that are important to him include "learning about diamonds" and "choosing a diamond." Delivered to the Leo Diamond Web site via these keywords, David finds text that includes his keywords, as well as other trigger words that relate to his particular needs. Remember, David is a Methodical—he cares about being educated and informed; he wants to feel competent. He does not want to pay too much. We've italicized his keywords and trigger words in the samples below:

> *How do I choose a diamond?*
>
> *How to buy* the best diamond at the *best price*: A step-by-step guide to *learning about diamonds* and becoming an *educated diamond consumer.*
>
> There's a lot more to buying a diamond than being in love. It's a *big investment* and an *important decision*! Before you make it, you should do the *research* just as you would before buying stock, or real estate, or an automobile for that matter.
>
> A *diamond education* doesn't cost you anything. But if you don't *learn about diamonds* before you select one, it could *cost you* a bundle. Your goal should be to approach the diamond counter as an *educated consumer.* That way, you can not only make an *informed, competent, and rational purchase,* but one that will *please the woman* in your life with its brilliance and beauty.

Makes sense, right? We're speaking his language using words that describe his needs, problems, and the solutions he is seeking. But wait a minute—*"please the woman"*—that doesn't sound like a rational methodical trigger word. That sounds awfully emotional—even romantic. How does that fit into David Commonsense's buying process?

"Pleasing the woman" is David's motivation. All the other keywords and trigger words speak to his needs. But his deepest motivation is to get her to say "Yes!" He genuinely wants to please her. It's true—he needs to make a very educated, logical decision about buying an engagement ring. But at the end of they day, it is his motivation, his love for this young lady, that will ultimately drive him to make the purchase.

Keywords indicate readiness

The specificity of a query can indicate the buyer's readiness to take action, according to a research study by Internet Retailer.

> The portal search sites - AOL, MSN and Yahoo - tend to get more simple search queries, in contrast to Google, where more complex search queries tend to be made. And **the more specific the term, the more likely (in the short term) that it will result in a direct conversion**, according to comScore. [emphasis ours]
>
> However, while specific terms have higher immediate conversion rates, users of broader search terms may well end up making a purchase later online, or even offline, based on their online research.[2]

A person who types in a very specific term—"Sony XBR Plasma TV"—is probably later in the buying cycle. In other words, this is someone who has a pretty good idea what he wants and is closer to making a purchase.

The person who types in a broad term—"big-screen TVs"—is probably earlier in the buying process. She hasn't narrowed down her search to a specific type or model of TV. She wants to know about her choices—she's still exploring options. But just because this visitor may not convert right away does not mean she is not valuable. If you can provide her with helpful information, if you can help her narrow down her choices, if you can help her feel confident in her decision, she may convert—either online or offline—at a later time. By answering her questions at this early stage in the buying process, you can start a relationship with her that may end up in a sale.

Sorting motivations and modalities

Just because you can design a particular persona does not mean you necessarily want to. You may decide that the person searching on "cheapest" is not the sort of customer with whom you wish to carry on a dialog. It's perfectly legitimate to limit your universe of buyers as you see fit.

Armed with all the knowledge that was uncovered, it is then the Persuasion Architect's job to begin the process of sorting out these different motivations and modalities into distinct buckets that will help us create our personas.

Bringing Personas to Life

John Steinbeck wrote, "Your audience is one single reader. I have found that sometimes it helps to pick out one person—a real person you know, or an imagined person—and write to that one."[1]

It isn't an accident that when we sit down and write a letter or e-mail to real people it is more personable, vital, and interesting than writing, say, a press release. It is much easier to write copy that comes alive when writing to a real person rather than a generic one.

Think about it this way. Imagine you have thirty seconds to sell a product to a person you can't see, have never met, and know nothing about. You probably start rattling off product features and those benefits that you'd find interesting. Because you don't know much about the person you're talking to, you tend to focus more on the product than the person.

Now, try to sell your best friend on that same product in thirty seconds. You know this person; you know what she likes and doesn't like. You're more animated. You can speak to her using language and hot buttons that are meaningful to her. Your presentation is very different, because this time, your focus is your friend.

Which sale do you think will be more successful?

This is why creating personas is so important, not only to your writing but to every communication you have with your customers. When you communicate with "average customers," your communications sound average and not very inspiring. But when you can speak to different customers in their own languages about what matters most to them, they *hear* you! They feel like you're speaking directly to them, not some abstract person with a wallet. They feel understood and valued.

The application of personas can enhance every customer communication you have, from your Web site, to ad copy, to e-mails, to customer service.

Empathy

The secret to creating personas is creating "real" people with whom everyone involved in managing your persuasive system can empathize. Empathy is the ultimate value of a persona, from which all else flows. Note we use "empathy" rather than "sympathy."

Whereas "sympathy" implies taking on another's beliefs, "empathy" involves merely understanding those beliefs. When you empathize with people, you actually appeal to their strengths and acknowledge them for who they are, not who you think they should be. James T. Hardee, MD, writes:

> Empathy is concerned with a much higher order of human relationship and understanding: engaged detachment. In empathy, we "borrow" another's feelings to observe, feel, and understand them—but not to take them onto ourselves. By being a participant-observer, we come to understand how the other person feels. An empathetic observer enters into the equation and then is removed.[2]

This is what empathy means to us, and why we consider it the ultimate purpose of persona creation. Of course, we all want to achieve our business goals. But the truth is we won't achieve our goals until our customers achieve theirs first. Empathy allows us to develop and articulate respect for our audience, which allow us to view and treat their needs as perfectly valid, regardless of whether we see it their way or agree with them. Empathy is the foundation for solid relationships, or as Rick said to Captain Renault in *Casablanca*, "Louis, I think this is the start of a beautiful friendship."

A framework for character development

Early on, we approached persona development as an intuitive process. But as it became clear that we were evolving a reproducible process, we systematized our intuitive processes, continued our research, and codified our results.

As part of this process, we wanted to find a systematic way to create personas that were rich, deep, believable, and not stereotypical. We looked to other groups that face the same problem and found a perfect match in fiction writers—we turned to the crafts of literature and film for insight into character development. Fortunately, we were introduced to the preeminent Hollywood screenwriting teacher, David Freeman.

Character Diamonds

Freeman taught us about "Character Diamonds" in his workshop "Beyond Structure."[3] The discussions of "Character Diamonds" and "Masks" below come from Freeman's ideas. Their applicability for creating personas as a marketing tool will quickly become apparent.

Freeman describes characters as a series of layers. One layer is the Character Diamond, which combines the traits that govern a character's personality. Freeman calls it a "Diamond" because a major character in a film possesses an average of four core personality traits—though some have three or five traits.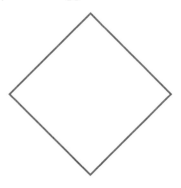

Each corner of the diamond represents a major trait in the character's personality, and each trait helps shape how the character sees the world, speaks, thinks, and acts.

For instance, let's say a character is (1) charming, (2) anxious, (3) driven, and (4) highly committed to his friends and family. These traits would be the corners of his Character Diamond.

For some characters, their personalities are spread evenly among their traits. But other characters might have an extremely powerful trait that eclipses all others. Although he obviously possesses other traits, Darth Vader's creepy evilness is by far his most dominant.

In his class, Freeman examines a character from *American Beauty:* Teenager Ricky Fitts, who is in love with Jane Burnham, daughter of Lester, the main character.

Ricky's character diamond looks like this:

- **Aesthetic/spiritual.** At one point, Ricky talks about a plastic bag dancing around him in the wind. It made him realize there's a benevolent life force behind all things. He also is keenly aware of beauty and discusses it several times.

- **Depressed/apathetic.** Ricky became depressed and apathetic after his father put him in a mental institution and drugged him for two years for being disobedient. He's fascinated by death. He talks about it regularly. He videotapes a dead bird. He offers no resistance when his father beats him. Ricky is apathetic; he rarely touches Jane, his girlfriend. He prefers to look at life, even at her in one scene, through the detached lens of a video camera.

- **Direct/unflinching.** Ricky stares at people with whom he interacts; nothing makes him flinch.

- **Irresponsible.** He smokes a lot of dope and deals it as well.

Ricky's four traits determine how he views things around him, as well as his decisions and interactions. As often happens in a film, some (but not all) of Ricky's traits change by the end. His depression lifts a bit as he becomes angry and rebellious enough to break free of his father's control. As this happens, a more engaged and responsible attitude begins to replace his irresponsibility.

Masks

Sometimes Character Diamond traits reveal apparent contradictions. Ricky's spiritual enlightenment seems in opposition to his irresponsibility. We can understand this in terms of what Freeman calls a "Mask." A Mask is a phony trait, a false self that fools others and sometimes even the character himself.

Thus, Ricky really does believe he's spiritually evolved. At first we in the audience see him the same way, until the contradictions in his character become evident.

Ricky's spiritual insights are a fundamental part of who he is, but they and his enlightened posturing are also a Mask—a phony personality—that covers his depression and irresponsibility.

Some Masks are totally phony (like the apparently happy "class clown" who's actually quite depressed). Others, like Ricky's, contain a degree of truth about the person.

Addressing a buyer's Mask

When creating your customers' personas, you must understand, and potentially address, any Masks those personas might wear.

Freeman offers these examples:

Players. White kids are the biggest consumers of rap music. Therefore, a suburban white kid may wear the Mask of an urban black kid. In the video games business, suburban white kids are often addressed as if they were inner-city black kids. A top-selling game in late 2004, *Grand Theft Auto: San Andreas,* allows gamers to role-play as a young urban black man in trouble with the law. White kids bought the game in record numbers—it really spoke to them (or at least it spoke to their Mask—the person they saw themselves to be, like Ricky Fitts seeing himself as enlightened.)

Road warriors. BMW pushes its "Ultimate Driving Machine" to men who usually end up driving 40 mph in rush-hour traffic. Yet these men view themselves as mighty conquerors of a glorious asphalt horizon, roaring full throttle through life and leaving testosterone in their wake.

BMW is not selling to physical reality; they are selling to the emotional reality of this Mask. The full picture is actually a little more complicated. This BMW persona's Character Diamond looks like this. He

- Views himself as powerful, a leader. He wants his car to reflect this. (This is the Character Diamond trait that is a Mask; the character doesn't have to be a powerful leader, but he does need to view himself as one.)
- Likes recognition for being rich and important. On some level, he feels he needs more recognition.
- Likes to go his own way in the world—not a follower.
- Is intelligent.

Just as Ricky Fitts' Mask is part true and part phony, so too are some BMW drivers' Masks. Some drivers really *are* conquerors—just not on the road.

The problem with being a world conqueror who sits behind a desk and wields a mighty keyboard is that no one knows you are one. It may be illegal to set speed records on the interstate, but that doesn't diminish the symbolic value of your BMW: you have the power to lay waste to your opponents.

For this Mask to work as a factor in a marketing campaign, it has to be part of the Character Diamond of your persona. That is, it has to resonate as some form of reality for the person who wears it.

Empathetic thinking: avoiding condescension

This BMW conqueror persona admittedly feels cliché. We in marketing could easily look down at him, minimizing or mocking his needs. You could imagine a copywriter with this attitude generating some pretty trite copy that could turn off buyers.

Your customers, obviously, are as complex as you are. Their struggles to forge good lives possess nobility and importance. When you are sensitive to this, you can generate empathy. Behind every Mask is some kind of pain, and that's why it's so easy to empathize with people's Masks.

Take those white kids who bought *Grand Theft Auto*. Many teens feel angry and stifled; they feel they're ready to make their mark in the world but don't know how to do it, nor will anyone give them permission. When you feel like an outsider, a black ex-convict (who might have been framed) can be a perfect symbol.

Can you empathize with these teens? Can you remember having similar feelings yourself when you were younger?

Let's look at the the BMW owner's second Character Diamond trait: He wants recognition. What does this mean to our persona? What kind of recognition does he seek? Why does he want it?

This kind of trait is more complex than simpler traits such as happy, athletic, rational, or playful. As a Mask, it covers pain—or as Freeman explains it, covers a psychological or emotional "fear, limitation, block, or wound" (FLBW). Understanding this allows us to develop compassion, which helps us communicate respect for the customer.

If you were creating a marketing campaign for BMW, you'd probably want to address the trait of being "powerful" in the following personas:

- A person who truly is powerful. For him, the BMW isn't a Mask. His business success depends on others treating him as powerful, and he needs all the public symbols he can muster as a form of branding.

- A person who is powerful but doesn't feel powerful. The BMW symbol of power is a reminder of who he is.

- A person who isn't powerful but works hard to be. The BMW symbolizes his professional ambition and may symbolize how he'd like to remold his personality.

- A person who will likely never be powerful. The BMW helps him see himself as powerful.

If you want to persuade each of these personas, you must be able to empathize with them. Can you find something in each of them that you understand and can appreciate—perhaps with which you even can identify?

The feeling of compassion, respect, and relationship you strive for isn't the intrusion of an emotion that bars your judgment. On the contrary, it's how you'll be able to judge well and market in ways that have your customers feeling appreciated and understood.

Developing these traits depends on careful uncovery. Incorporating Freeman's Character Diamond will be a key ingredient when you create personas. Character Diamonds help you create more human, believable personas. When you design a persuasive system, you must address the Character Diamond of each persona you want to reach. And that's leaps and bounds more useful to you than cardboard cutout "average users."

After the preliminary sorting of information—from demographic and business topology explorations—into different persona "piles," we begin fleshing out our personas. Here we apply our understanding of the sale's complexity (using Complexograms) and psychographics (preference and temperament), as well as construct our personas' Character Diamonds.

When we've done this, we have a firm handle on the words and processes we will need to work on for our personas. We understand the specific questions they will ask, and how we can answer those questions. We understand the needs and motivations for each persona. Armed with this knowledge, we can set about creating the structures that will help our personas build the confidence to buy as they move through our persuasive systems.

Best Buy's "Jill"

A dominant player in consumer electronics, Best Buy wants to make it easier for women who don't understand the technologies to shop with the company. They also want women to know the business isn't limited to consumer electronics.

So Best Buy created "Jill." Jill is a persona, a soccer mom who is motivated to please and care for her family. She doesn't want an intimidating experience when she shops for appliances or electronics. She needs to feel she has a friend along to help.

Even this relatively simple level of empathy lets Best Buy interact with Jill to consider needs and motivations they otherwise might have missed. Jill helps Best Buy to ask better questions:

- Does Jill know we carry toys?
- How will Jill know what toy or game is best for her kids?

- Would Jill know, or even care, about the different types of TVs we carry?

- How can we help Jill find what she needs without making her feel like she needs a technical degree?

- How does Jill want to buy appliances?

- What intimidates Jill about electronics?

- What will make Jill's trip to Best Buy or BestBuy.com more productive and less frustrating?

Jill can also help Best Buy create relevant messaging ("Hassle- and fear-free electronics shopping," "We speak English, not Tech," "We make electronics easy," "Tech-talk-free zones available," or "Kids play while you shop") and develop a unified multi-channel experience across their promotional mailings, Web site, and stores. By all accounts, Jill-based marketing has been an enormous hit with customers.

When she recently needed to replace her computer, Lisa made the trip to her local Best Buy. Aware her unfolding experience was influenced by a persona, Lisa struck up a conversation with her computer salesperson (a woman), and asked how the computer department felt about working with the Jill persona. Did the staff find it difficult? Had they been resistant to it? Was it working? Lisa's salesperson was genuinely enthusiastic about all the benefits.

But Lisa's conversation didn't stay one-on-one for very long. Others on the sales staff came to contribute their comments. It was like an impromptu, self-congratulatory celebration on the sales floor. One salesperson talked about how much he valued the in-store training on how to work with Jill—it helped him feel he could do his job better. Everyone was unilaterally supportive—even the manager of the in-house Geek Squad, who also dropped in on the conversation.

Delighted that the Best Buy store staff were addressing her concerns with remarkable sensitivity, making sure she understood exactly what was possible and why, Lisa bought her computer and took it home several hours later. That day, Lisa won (thanks, Jill!); the staff won; and Best Buy won.

Dealing with consensus

When we deal with situations involving personal or group consensus, we are often presented with tensions between possibly conflicting motivations. When more than one person is involved in a decision process, you need to take the other decision-makers into account.

Take the couple planning a vacation. She wants to incorporate a lot of physical activity or sightseeing into the experience, while he simply wants to park under a tree with a two-foot stack of books and stay there until it's time to board the plane back.

We once worked with a client who managed a rehabilitative program for troubled youth. Some of the customers were couples. The father wanted the child subjected to a healthy dose of "tough love" in a "boot camp" environment, while the mother was terrified her child would be traumatized.

In these situations, it is beneficial to describe the couple as a single persona that embraces the dynamics of this tension. Although each individual needs to be persuaded separately, the decision is made jointly.

Consider a Competitive software-purchasing agent. He must take into consideration his own criteria for choosing the software (price, installation, technical support). He must be aware of the CEO's criteria (meticulous documentation of how this will affect the bottom line). He must also be aware of end user criteria (ease of use and help desk support). As a Competitive, he only needs to see the big picture. But the other needs he must meet to satisfy everyone who will be affected by this decision will require him to draw on other preferences as well.

The one we want to go away

Then there's the "anti-persona." Sometimes we want to discourage those customers who demand huge chunks of our resources (both time and money) without yielding much (or any) profit. An "anti-persona" is a perfectly acceptable and often appropriate use for a persona. Best Buy has created an anti-persona to recognize those customer segments with which they would prefer not to deal.

Best Buy's "angels" are customers who boost profits at the consumer-electronics giant by snapping up high-definition television, portable electronics, and newly released DVDs without waiting for markdowns or rebates.

The "devils" are its worst customers. They buy products, apply for rebates, return the purchases, and then buy them back at returned-merchandise discounts. They load up on "loss leaders," severely discounted merchandise designed to boost store traffic, and then flip the goods at a profit on eBay. They slap down rock-bottom price quotes from Web sites and demand that Best Buy make good on its lowest-price pledge. "They can wreak enormous economic havoc," says [Brad] Anderson [Best Buy's CEO].[4]

Consultant Larry Selden, a professor at Columbia University's Graduate School of Business, persuaded Anderson to view his company "as a portfolio of customers, not product lines," to identify his profitable customers and then meet their needs better than the competition does. Best Buy identified different groups of angels: upper-income men ("Barrys"), suburban mothers ("Jills"), small business owners, young family men, and technology enthusiasts ("Buzzes"). Each store evaluates its local demographics and then chooses two of these angel groups. The store merchandises and markets to those groups. Best Buy staff receive training that helps them to identify "desirable customers according to their shopping preferences and behavior."[5] Early results indicate Best Buy's pilot stores are clobbering the competition.

To deter the devils, Best Buy is reinforcing a 15 percent restocking fee for returns, and reselling returned merchandise over the Internet rather than in the store of origin.

Best Buy's angel and devil personas are largely based on transactional and relational shopping modes. The company incorporates demographic information and behavioral cues. The only piece of the equation that seems missing at present is the psychographic dimension.

Who should create the personas?

We've mentioned that when it comes to gathering input for persona creation, everyone who has direct contact with your customers should be involved, especially sales staff and customer-service representatives.

However, not every person in an organization is equally helpful in creating personas. Our Persuasion Architects all share the same MBTI characteristic, and we highly encourage you to consider this when you make your choice. A good Persuasion Architect should possess strong intuition and feeling (NF) preferences. In other words, they should be individuals who fit the Humanistic profile we described in Chapter Twenty.

Humanistic people excel at empathizing. People who examine the interrelationships between character traits and the stages of the buying decision process, and then create the fleshed-out descriptions that bring personas to life so others can empathize with them, must be able to imagine themselves in the position of each persona. They must be sensitive to the nuances of relationships and the dynamics of emotional needs. They also need to be able to appreciate the bigger picture of how these pieces fit together.

When your goal is creating empathy, you want to turn to those people for whom big pictures and empathy are natural preferences. And that would be your Humanistics!

The art of storytelling

What's the best way to deliver a memorable, persuasive message? Tell a story. Don't believe us? How many copies did *"Who Moved My Cheese"* sell? Still remember *Aesop's Fables?* Look at the elements of a good story—characters, plot, conflict resolution—and you'll see a lot of similarities with Persuasion Architecture.

Creating personas is just like telling a story. It involves building the characters, creating a narrative plot, and stating the conflict or tension that requires resolving. We've already talked about how to build your characters. Your plot is based on what those characters are trying to accomplish—their end goals. The conflict and tension that require resolving are your customers' unanswered questions, their objections, and the friction in the buying and selling processes.

Your personas are your protagonists. It's the job of a Persuasion Architect to role-play every persona's experience, and it's our comprehensive understanding of this story that allows us to move into the next phase of wireframing.

The persona-creation process concludes by crafting the well-written narratives that describe in detail how each persona buys your product or service. It's a robust story that takes everything into account.

The narrative is filled with descriptions of how the protagonists began their buying processes: whom they are talking to, what they are thinking and feeling, what they encounter when they visit you and your competitors. It accounts for all possible interactions across all possible channels.

Our narrative confirms whether we've really hit the mark. Through these persona-specific narratives, we predict what actions a persona will take and why. We create pathways that align the buying process with the selling process. We establish a structure of measurable conversion points, the definable places we can reference when analyzing whether our predictive models were correct. In other words, we create plots that start with personas achieving their goals and end with businesses achieving their goals.

Creating the narrative

Family vacations can be stressful to plan; there's plenty of room for conflict. Suppose we wanted to reduce conflict and generate enthusiasm? We've recently been working with a well-known theme park. During uncovery, we identified a likely scenario where twelve-year-old Emily and ten-year-old John could identify the attractions they wanted to see. They could make a list to show their parents, "Hey, Mom and Dad—let's do this!" Excited by their upcoming vacation, Emily and John visit the Web site repeatedly. They create a wish list to make sure they don't miss a thing.

Their parents are excited by Emily and John's enthusiasm, but they also have their own agendas—Keith wants to play golf; Geri wants to spend time in a spa; they want an evening when they can have time alone together to enjoy the resort's nightlife. Because they all plan their trip together, they become increasingly confident this trip will be one that everyone enjoys. They're eager to make their reservations.

This story has a happy ending—family *and* theme park get what they want. As we told our story in uncovery, it was simple to imagine a Web-based collaboration tool and agenda-planner as important pieces in the buying process.

A well-created persona should leap off the page (or the computer screen) and feel like a real person. This should be someone you feel like you know very well. When you show your personas to your staff, they should respond, "Yeah, I know her—I talked to her the other day," and "Hey, I know that guy! That's my client, Joe!" That's when you know you've done the exercise correctly. And that's cause for a very big smile.

CHAPTER TWENTY-THREE

The Architecture Metaphor

U p to now, we've deconstructed the elements that make up the visions of the very best marketers today. It is not quite the equivalent of a paint-by-number Picasso. You've grasped the importance of uncovery. You've gained insight into who your customers are and how they operate. You have the framework for creating personas. These are the building blocks you need to create persuasive systems.

You now know your objectives; you may have a vision of the strategy. The crucial questiona are: How do you implement that strategy? How do you convey it to the rest of your team? How do you take your vision and translate it to everything from a billboard to a call center to a pay-per-click ad to a radio spot to an e-mail campaign and beyond?

A vision cannot be measured; a plan can. Plans allow you to translate overarching visions into individual steps. It's time for a blueprint. Because planning for experience is not a new concept, we turned to an architectural metaphor for our inspiration. A century ago, Frank Lloyd Wright wrote:

A building should contain as few rooms as will meet the condition which give it rise and under which we live, and which the architect should strive continually to simplify; the ensemble of the rooms should then be carefully considered that comfort and utility may go hand in hand with beauty.[1]

Frank Lloyd Wright focused on creating intimate experiences in space. Of course, we don't necessarily work with physical spaces: We work with cognitive processes (mental spaces). Specifically, our practice has worked with cognitive processes that take place online.

How do we design blueprints that build confidence and fuel persuasive momentum so that we build the same carefully crafted experience Frank Lloyd Wright talks about? The Internet was our vehicle for understanding how to translate the narrative of experience into an actual plan that mapped out a persuasive system.

The beauty of the Web is that everything is measurable. The frustration of the Web is that measuring *everything* can give you lots of noise, which drowns out the important signals. Online, the only thing you can really measure is a click; but every click is the end result of an unfolding cognitive process. Hyperlinks allow us to see and measure connections in action. They allow us to measure the effectiveness of our scenarios.

Frank Lloyd Wright's observations become relevant to us if we replace "building" with "Web site." Spinning out this analogy, "rooms" become Web pages and "doors" are calls to action. We could think of nature, "comfort and utility" as functionality. The "materials" we choose are not wood, brick, or stone; they are copy, images, and design templates.

Along the way, our clients encouraged us to take our persona scenario planning beyond the Web. The customers are the same; the cognitive processes are the same, even if you can't measure them by clicks. If you can map out a personal experience on a Web site, why can't you map it out in other mediums?

Here's how we would paraphrase Frank Lloyd Wright for the experience economy at large:

A persuasive system should contain as few persuasive entities as will meet the conditions that give it rise and under which we live and which the architect would strive continually to simplify; the ensemble of it should then be carefully considered that content and imagery go hand in hand with persuasiveness.

Independent of medium, every marketer faces the conceptual problem of how to plan scenarios and measure their effect—measurement of effect being the way we assess our return on investment. In designing any kind of scenario, there are three components we need to take into account:

- *The selling process*—our objectives. We can easily measure whether we have satisfied our selling process.

- *The buying process*—the customers' objectives. We can reasonably infer by measurement (we can't ever *really* know) whether we have satisfied some or all of the phases in the buying process. We only know we have probably satisfied their buying process when customers actually complete our selling process.

- *Time*—the connections between cause and effect are not always straightforward. It's entirely possible that the customer who took a deciding action a few minutes ago has been paying attention to your messages, quietly, for over a year. Only time enables you to differentiate an abandoned decision from a pending outcome.

Using Persuasion Architecture allows you to implement your vision by creating "visible forms" and shaping the "aesthetic qualities" of your persuasive systems. It's how you plan your rooms and your schemes of interior decoration, how you benefit from the shifting patterns of sunlight through windows, and how your rooms relate to each other to support the flow of human exchange. Think of each of these as customer touch points. Through our persuasive systems, we want to recreate the same intimate experience Frank Lloyd Wright considered essential in the design of physical spaces.

In order to attain our goal of intimacy and the perception of a personalized experience, we use a methodology called *wireframing*. Execution is always the hardest part in translating visions. Persuasion Architecture provides the framework to map them out.

CHAPTER TWENTY-FOUR

Wireframing As an Interactivity Map

B ack to our three questions:

1. Who are we trying to persuade to take the action?

2. What is the action we want someone to take?

3. What does that person need in order to feel confident taking that action?

We've dug deeply into the matter of whom we are trying to persuade. Now we can begin to deal systematically with the actions we want our personas to take, and what they need so they feel comfortable taking that action. Actions and needs establish the parameters of our interaction.

We want to create a map of that interaction, through planned scenarios that acknowledge and meet every opportunity. This is the process of wireframing.[1]

A context for relevance

In recent years, businesses have been experiencing what we might call "The Google Effect." The year 2000 was roughly the watershed in search engine development for delivering relevance. Remember, every time you type a keyword or phrase into a search engine, you are asking a question. You expect a relevant answer—one that gives you the information you are looking for. For instance, if you type in "Paris Hilton engagement," you expect results that link to information about Paris Hilton getting engaged, not how to get engaged while in Paris at a Hilton hotel.

Google upped the ante for every commercial media experience in which we participate. We quickly came to expect that our questions—and not simply our search engine questions—would be answered with relevant information.

If you "up the ante," you increase the importance or value of something. The stake, or investment, gets larger. As people begin to embrace developments and innovations, their expectations increase. Compact discs upped the ante for sound quality across all recording media—and as we became accustomed to superior sound quality, soon we began to expect it.

Relevance, however, isn't a simple, binary matter. Relevance is relative; it depends on the angle from which we approach the information. Relevance is in the eye of the beholder. Therefore, we need to address relevance in terms of the customer, because the customer is not necessarily going to define relevance as we define it.

Relevance is as much about the context of a situation as it is about the facts themselves. Sometimes meaning is comprehensible *only* when you understand the context. "Who's your daddy?" means one thing when a teacher asks it of a child waiting to be picked up from school, but in different circumstances, the question can mean something altogether different. Ask the question to an adult woman, and you're probably asking about the man who is spending lots of money on her. Ask the question to a Brit, and you're probably inquiring about the person's boss. Knowing to whom you are talking makes all the difference when you are trying to communicate relevance.

We can tell you trigger words are critical to communicating relevance to your customer, but how can you know which trigger words to use without understanding the context of use? *Advantage* can be a good trigger word for a persona in Competitive mode, but it will fall on deaf ears or eyes, as the case may be, for a person in Humanistic mode.

Wireframing is about mapping context with relevance.

Mapping interactivity provides you with the context for how people will navigate your persuasive system. It's the way you make sure your customers have the relevant, persuasive information they need to proceed.

Waypoints and points of resolution: building persuasive momentum

We also have to understand that as we are mapping context with relevance, we are building an experience of persuasive momentum. We are fueling the interest and desire of AIDAS, communicating enthusiasm, and building confidence.

Now that we understand the phases of the selling process and the buying decision process, the first step in executing a plan requires separating the elements of the persuasive system. Waypoints are the steps that provide forward momentum in the selling process. Points of resolution are the detours a customer may take to get his questions answered during the buying decision process.

We have already established that customers are not interested in our selling process except to the extent it fits into their buying decision process. As we create the narrative of our scenarios, we need to plot waypoints and points of resolution that fit with the customers' agendas rather than our own. As customers gain resolve through investigating their points of resolution, we must anticipate and plan for returning the customer to our sales process in a way that feels natural to their buying decision process. In planning for this return, we provide "resolving doors" that resolve the customer's questions—and revolve him back into our sales process.

In practice on the Web

Using a Web site as an example (a Web site can be a fully contained scenario experience), let's look at how we articulate waypoints and points of resolution. On a Web site, wireframing marries your sales process to the customers' buying decision processes through the use of specific hyper-links that create and sustain persuasive momentum. Calls to action are the type most people are familiar with. These are the forward-moving impera-tives of your sales process. However, far too many Web sites fail to use points of resolution, hyperlinks that address questions and concerns spe-cific to your customers' buying decision processes.

Calls to action. Each step in your sales process requires a customer to take a specific action. Contained within waypoints, calls to action are the hyperlinks that move your customer through your sales process—they give customers the opportunity to take the action you want them to take. These are the links that are critical to you, the ones you want your cus-tomers to click on.

Calls to action are *sales process links*. We create them by pairing an imperative verb with an implied benefit:

- Locate a retailer near you
- Subscribe to our newsletter
- Compare service plans

Points of resolution. Depending on where they are in the buying deci-sion process, your customers need answers to specific questions before they can make a decision. You must help them resolve these questions before you can proceed with the sales process. The nature of the questions depends on the persona—not all personas will require the same information.

Points of resolution are the hyperlinks that answer the customers' questions. These links, which have no hierarchical value, help customers resolve sticking points in the buying decision process. A customer is never required to click on a point of resolution to move through the sales process; these links simply let customers collect the information they need to feel confident making a decision.

Points of resolution are *buying decision process links*. We create them using nouns and place them on pages where customers are most likely to ask that particular question. Very often, points of resolution are embedded-text links—they appear within blocks of descriptive or explanatory copy.

A customer who isn't interested in the linked information needn't follow the link.

- "You might be surprised by all the industries that have discovered ways to use grommets."
- "Grommets have improved greatly due to new grommet technology."

Resolving Doors. A point of resolution hyperlink takes your prospect to a resolution page where the question is answered with relevant information. A resolution page can offer additional point of resolution hyperlinks—so a path through resolution pages can seem circular—hence "resolving" door, like a hotel lobby revolving door.

With resolving doors you can offer your customer the opportunity to ask another question, and you always offer a way for your customer to return to the sales process. Think of the nightmare scenario where you're stuck in one of those revolving doors and can't get out. Never lead your customers into a dead end!

If at any time, on any resolution page, the customer feels his questions have been answered and he is ready to exit, he should find carefully worded hyperlinks leading him back into your sales process. These exit links, worded as a call to action, relate more to the sales process than the buying process—they introduce your specific solutions to the questions he is asking.

What may look like almost random behavior on the part of the buyer, within their context, is usually fairly predictable. Walking a mile in the persona's shoes, we can ask ourselves, "What is it that we still don't know at this stage of our buying process? What do we need to know? What would clinch the deal? What's the deal-killer for us?"

Each step of the sales process, just like each step of the buying process, is a micro-action. At all points of interactivity, which are the touch points within our persuasive system, we have to ask ourselves the same three questions—what action, who takes it, and what do they need in order to do it? With each subsequent step, we let customers know we are providing them with increasing degrees of relevance. At each point, we want to help the customer know where they are and how they can move forward.

Persuasion entities

Points of interactivity—touch points—occur throughout a persuasive system and take many forms: a Web page, an e-mail, a snail-mail letter, a banner ad, an out-bound telemarketing call, a billboard, a television commercial, the packaging of a product, a sales conversation . . . whatever medium you choose to engage your audience.

How do you know which medium is the most effective for a particular message to a particular customer? By mapping the cognitive process of the buyer first, we can determine what persuasion entity will best satisfy the goal. The interactive map helps us to begin sorting these details.

Within the constellation of persuasion entities available to you, there are push entities and there are pull entities. (Contrary to the prevailing hoopla, we do not believe push marketing is facing extinction. But as the opportunities for pull marketing increase, the context of push marketing will need to adapt.) There is an appropriate time and place for each, and you need to know when it's more valuable to use one over the other.

In the wireframing tool we have developed as part of our Persuasion Architecture MAPsuite of software applications, we refer to two types of actions. *Explicit actions* are pull actions—the customer takes the initiative. *Implicit actions* are push actions—permission-based ways marketers reach out without directly asking.

Clicking on a hyperlink that says "Sign up for our monthly newsletter" is an explicit action. The customer is invited to take action and sign up for the newsletter. The auto-responder you send her after she signs up is an implicit action: You take the initiative by sending her an e-mail. This could be an e-mail confirming and thanking her for signing up for the newsletter—perhaps you also inform her of special offers or upcoming events.

Choosing an entity

Persuasion entities each have their own characteristics—an e-mail is different from a letter, which is different from a sales conversation. The dynamics of context and appropriate choices have to do with how the customer comes to the entity. Each entity—whether a TV ad, banner ad, or Google AdWord—sets up a different expectation, will be seen in a different context, and will likely trigger different responses.

For example, our reaction to an untargeted banner ad served up as run-of-site, inviting us to check out a new product, would be very different from our reaction to a highly targeted search that produced a very specific and highly relevant result on a search engine result page. The important distinction lies in our expectation of relevance. When we're invited in a general sort of way to check out something new, we may not want all the details right away, but if we've made a very specific inquiry, we expect to be presented with a very specific set of results.

A Persuasion Architect's job is to map the cognitive processes that are going to help customers reach the goal that is both theirs and ours. This may bring to mind the idea of pull marketing, because we are suggesting pulling people along by their own motivation. While we have their interest, while we are being relevant, we are pulling them along with a rope. Without their interest, it would be very hard to push that rope.

Many discussions these days about "pull" marketing are oversimplifications of a valid concept that allows customers to do things for their own reasons. We would prefer to say the frameworks available in Persuasion Architecture create a persuasive model of voluntary momentum rather than a coercive model. This isn't about manipulating someone to do something you want them to do. It's about providing relevant information of genuine interest that lets buyers choose their own path. It isn't about control; it's about choice.

CHAPTER TWENTY-FIVE

Architecting a Persuasion Scenario

We've used the word *scenario* as we've talked about personas and wireframing. Many people intuitively understand what is meant by the word. A scenario is a kind of story, an outline of a plot for a novel or a play. But beyond that, depending on whom you ask, you can get entirely different explanations for the word.

If you were to ask an analyst to define *scenario*, that person would probably talk about a "funnel," as well as the linear series of binary events a customer must take to complete the funnel process. Either the customer takes the prescribed action, or he doesn't.

A salesperson would define *scenario* a bit differently. Having an intuitive sense of how a customer would buy in a specific situation, a salesperson thinks of narrating a non-linear sales script of how a customer might participate in a conversion action.

So which explanation is correct? The correct answer is "neither." The better answer is "both." Analysts and salespeople have legitimate, mission-critical reasons to define *scenario* differently. The salesperson must account for the needs of the customer; the analytics expert must be able to meas-ure the success or failure of a scenario effectively. But taken individually, their definitions fall short.

Taken together, their definitions provide the essential elements for describing exactly what a scenario is and what it must accomplish.

A scenario consists of persuasive components that lead a customer to participate in a conversion action. Some of these components will be linear; others will be non-linear. All must be customer-focused—based on how each customer approaches the decision to buy—rather than business-focused.

A scenario provides a structure for the meaningful measure-ment of customer activity so you can optimize performance.

Components of the persuasion scenario

When we explicitly plan a scenario to meet the needs of marketers, analysts, *and* customers, we call it a "persuasion scenario." It helps to understand the components that make up this beast.

Driving point. This is the prospecting point, *outside the funnel*, where a scenario begins. It might be a search engine result, a pay-per-click ad, a print ad, or any number of persuasion entities. It may also be the result of branding or a recommendation—things that don't give us the benefit of direct evidence so we can understand their intentions. For our purposes in defining a scenario, however, the driving point is the place where the customer shows a level of interest in entering the scenario, even if we can't always measure it.

The reason you must establish a driving point when describing a sce-nario is to understand the customer's angle of approach. Knowing the angle of approach gives you better insight into the customer's motivation.

Think of it as the for-sale sign (measurable) in front of a house or a phone call from a neighbor (not measurable)—the driving point is not the house itself, but the persuasive alert that the house is available.

Funnel points. These are *entries to the conversion funnel*—a door (perhaps one of many) to the house that's for sale. At this point, you, the business, are in a position to control and develop the dynamic of the persuasive process. A funnel point might be a landing page or main product category page, which essentially functions as a home page would to build persuasive momentum within the scenario itself. For a scenario to be measurable, we must be able to identify the funnel point.

In our house analogy, think of the funnel point as making contact with the person selling the home.

Points of resolution. These are your opportunities to provide the information customers may need to answer questions associated with their individual buying processes. Each point of resolution must always connect to a waypoint or a conversion beacon (see below) to ensure the customer never misses an opportunity to convert.

Think of points of resolution as the questions a potential house buyer would ask about the neighbors, the schools, or local shopping opportunities.

Waypoints. These are "persuasive touch points"—points of interactivity—that are integral to the seller's conversion goals but critical to the needs of a particular customer. Waypoints support the sales process and the conversion goal.

For example, a Methodical, price-conscious homebuyer would certainly wonder about costs, so a waypoint might be a document that would answer questions about taxes and maintenance costs for the house.

Points of resolution and waypoints are persuasive components that support the non-linear qualities of the online experience. The order in which a customer hits these points and the actual number of points she interacts with is dynamic. In other words, both allow her to interact with you in a way that feels comfortable to her.

In all this, however, there is a danger in mistaking movement as forward momentum. When we are developing scenarios, we have to be careful not simply to move customers around the information; we must always be trying to move them forward toward their goal.

Conversion beacon. A conversion beacon signals the first (or next) step in a linear process through which a customer must pass to reach the conversion point. Points of resolution and waypoints lead a customer to the conversion beacon, the place where the customer demonstrates the intention to convert.

To persuade customers to make an offer on the home, points of resolution and waypoints would build value for the home; the preparation of an offer would constitute the first conversion beacon. Each step in completing the offer process constitutes another conversion beacon—and the customer must complete each step in order.

In a store, you may enter the conversion beacon when you go to stand at the checkout line, even though you have yet to complete the purchase. Checkout processes for online retail Web sites usually include several conversion beacons.

Conversion point. This is the point where we know with absolute certainty that a customer has successfully completed a persuasion scenario. The conversion point is the entity that gets delivered so that both the customer and the business know conversion has taken place. This entity is usually some form of confirmation.

When the offer for the home is conveyed to the seller, one scenario is now complete (although there are additional scenarios required before the macro-conversion goal of purchasing the home is complete).

Persuasion scenarios in action

Each component of a persuasion scenario is designed with a customer focus that acknowledges the differing needs of each customer segment, depending on where each is in the buying decision process, and provides persuasive momentum. Into that structure, and always sensitive to it, the scenario incorporates the sales process of the business in a way that benefits customers without undermining their buying decision process.

This explicit planning provides exceptional support for the analytic expert's goal of measuring so marketers and salespeople can, in turn, optimize.

Linear aspects. The analytics expert describes the success of the linear aspect of a scenario. Linear aspects typically occur at the beginning or at the end of a conversion process.

At the beginning, they could look like this:

Search engine result (driving point) to landing page (funnel point)

or

Banner ad (driving point) to landing page (funnel point)

or

A flier (driving point) to a store (funnel point)

And at the end:

Shopping cart (conversion beacon) to complete checkout (conversion point)

or

Form completion (conversion beacon) to confirmation (conversion point)

or

Taking the product to the checkout counter (conversion beacon) to receiving a purchase receipt (conversion point)

Linear aspects of a scenario come into play when customers need to start a conversion process or complete a registration process or checkout process. Measurement for these aspects is relatively straightforward.

Non-linear aspects. Intuitive marketers and salespeople know customers don't always interact in such linear fashion. Many times customers have questions that need to be resolved before they can buy. Answering these questions requires building non-linear qualities into the scenario—these are more difficult, but by no means impossible, to measure.

Customers define the non-linear aspects of a scenario as they navigate your persuasion entities. These scenarios can be explicitly planned or implicit; they do occur randomly even if they were not planned. In a non-linear scenario, you can measure the point at which the customer starts the scenario (driving point) to the point at which they complete the intended scenario (conversion point), identifying whether or not the customer hits the key value waypoints.

In online persuasive systems, Web analytics can identify the click-through path within the non-linear points of resolution. This helps marketers determine whether they are providing the appropriate content to maintain persuasive momentum.

The Web is particularly valuable in that it can function as a low-cost testing laboratory in which you can evaluate the effectiveness of messaging you'd like to apply online and offline.

Sample scenarios

How might scenarios play out in real-world situations? We asked one of our Persuasion Architects, Anthony "Shaq" Garcia, to help us illustrate. Anthony would like you to meet Susan.

Susan is married to George and the mother of three. She works outside the home full-time and is expecting a hard-earned bonus. With a portion of that bonus, Susan wants to surprise her family—particularly George—with a big-screen television. But Susan does not consider herself techno-savvy. To her, these sorts of television are simply big, beautiful (and expensive) luxuries. She doesn't understand the differences between rear-projection, plasma, HDTV, and screen formats. She wants her family to be thrilled, but she also wants to make sure she makes an intelligent purchase. (This presentation of Susan is a profile, not a fully fleshed-out persona.)

Scenario #1: gathering information. Susan knows she'll eventually visit a showroom, but first she wants to learn more about her big-screen options so she can narrow her choices. In this scenario, the goal is to help change the angle of Susan's perception early in her buying process. You can measure the success of this micro-conversion scenario (the point of which is not necessarily an actual purchase) by looking at whether Susan accesses a store-locator tool, examining how she interacts with various points of resolution, determining how much time she spends with way-points, and whether she downloads information documents.

The path of Susan's information-gathering scenario might look like this:

- Susan begins by going to a search engine and searching on the key phrase "how to buy a big screen TV." The search results constitute the driving point for Susan's scenario.
- Susan selects the search result for a consumer electronics Web site that is filled with common sense, plainspoken language about big-

screen TVs and how to buy them. This is a funnel point for Susan's scenario.

- While she is reading the information the business provides, Susan identifies a resource on this Web site that seems extremely helpful—this is a waypoint. Here she learns about the relevant benefits of each feature as well as about how to spot quality. The information also discusses extended warranties.

- Susan considers buying a complete home theater system and looks at a few prepackaged options, gathering more information about what she might need and what she can expect to get for her budget. Each of these investigations constitutes a point of resolution in Susan's scenario.

- Impressed with her experience interacting with this Web site, Susan wonders if there's a brick-and-mortar arm of this business near her. This step serves as a conversion beacon. Other conversion beacons will herald each step she needs to take before she gets an answer to her question.

- Susan gets a list of all the stores in her area. This is the conversion point. Susan has completed her information-gathering scenario.

Often, the conversion point of one scenario is the driving point for another scenario. In this example, the list of local stores (conversion point) Susan reaches at the end of her information-gathering scenario becomes the driving point of another scenario later in her buying process where she goes to visit one of the stores on the list.

Scenarios can have influencers. Suppose George discovers Susan is planning to buy a big-screen television for the family. He worries that sales staff might take Susan for a ride, but he also wants to make sure she gets the model with all the features he wants. Susan wants to reassure George she is being thorough, and now that he knows about her plan, she would like his input.

We would need to decide if the Susan/George dynamic required a specific Susan/George scenario, complete with its specific conversion point.

But in the Susan scenario, where she's gathering the information and making the decisions, we can help her address George's concerns through a point of resolution. For example, we might offer a "What he wants in his big-screen TV" Web page she can share with him.

Scenario #2: zeroing-in. Behind the scenes, Susan has been researching her planned purchase online and visiting several offline stores. She has decided she wants a plasma display and is ready to compare apples to apples.

The success of this scenario depends on getting Susan quickly to information she requires about the specific type of product she wants. Here, downloads of information, even an "add-to-cart" click (regardless of whether Susan actually completes the purchase), can indicate successful micro-conversions.

- Susan visits a few consumer review Web sites (the reviews might also come through the business). She's getting a sense of which manufacturer and model would offer her the best value (driving points).
- Susan compares specific models by visiting Sony's and Samsung's Web sites (funnel point and waypoints).
- Susan checks out the descriptions and pictures (points of resolution).
- Susan downloads a PDF of this information (conversion beacon).
- Susan receives confirmation that her PDF download was successful (conversion point).

It is entirely possible in this sort of scenario that Susan's path will take her away from the information you, as the consumer electronics business, might want her to see. Your ability to address all of Susan's concerns within the context of *your* persuasion entity will help Susan build confidence in your ability to meet her needs. Remember, she'll look for the information; you have to choose whether or not you provide it.

Scenario #3: ad-driven offline purchase. Susan sees an advertisement (a "push" persuasion entity) for a television she wasn't aware of. The price point and the specifications are within her parameters. Susan may have come in contact with this information through a television ad, a radio spot, a banner ad, a catalog, an e-mail, or a specific piece of promotional material sent to her via snail-mail.

This scenario usually takes place completely offline, as part of a combined media effort. However, in Susan's mind it connects with, and is evaluated in light of, the research she has been doing and the positive or negative experiences she has collected along the way. The business goal for this advertisement is to direct Susan to the place where she can make the purchase.

- Susan sees an advertisement for a television she wasn't aware of (driving point).
- Susan visits the store (funnel point).
- Susan engages a salesperson with specific questions about the television. She also asks about manufacturer's warranties and whether the business offers an extended warranty (waypoints).
- Susan questions the salesperson about various ways to situate the television in her home, and examines mounting solutions as well as entertainment centers (points of resolution).
- Susan asks the salesperson to pull the equipment and accessories she will need (conversion beacon).
- Susan goes to the checkout counter with her order to pay for those items (conversion beacon).
- Susan pays for her items and gets her receipt (conversion point).

Scenario #4: returning purchase. Susan has purchased the television she felt best met her family's needs. Everyone loves it, and now she'd like to consider adding a home theater system. She doesn't want to spend a lot of time shopping, as she figures it will be easy to upgrade the sound later if she wants. She doesn't see this as a critical or complex purchase— she simply wants a system that is compatible and gets the job done.

- Susan visits the consumer electronics Web site for the brick-and-mortar store where she purchased her television—the one she initially visited to locate the store (driving point).

- Susan looks for a high-level page for home theater systems (funnel point).

- Susan peruses the bestsellers. One seems like a bargain unit, but another looks as though it might work better with her television. However, the picture makes her think the color of the home theater system won't match the color of her television. She finds the product page for the specific television she bought to get another look at it, as well as examines the home theater system's product page to see if it is offered in different colors (waypoints).

- On her television's product page, Susan notices a "recommended accessories" link and clicks (waypoint).

- Susan sees a plug-and-play home theater system that is the same brand as her television, matches it, and is within her budget. She adds the home theater system to her shopping cart (conversion beacon).

- Susan reviews her shopping cart and clicks "continue" (conversion beacon).

- Susan enters her personal information and clicks "continue" (conversion beacon).

- Because shipping costs have not been displayed, Susan becomes curious about them. She clicks on a "shipping options" link and reviews her choices (point of resolution).

- Susan proceeds to payment information (conversion beacon).

- Susan enters her payment information, chooses the second-day shipping option, and clicks "continue" (conversion beacon).

- Susan gets to the order summary page, where she is asked to confirm the purchase, and clicks on "place my order" (conversion beacon).

- Susan waits for the confirmation page to appear (conversion point).

The whole enchilada?

Because people have a tendency to think of conversion as a function of the macro-level goal, it's easy to conclude that a scenario is a framework for the buying decision process start to finish. For extremely simple sales and buying decision processes, this might be true. And for those to-die-for customers who know exactly what they want, a single scenario may be sufficient for a business to secure the macro-level conversion in one go. Certainly a cut-to-the-chase scenario is essential for these customers.

Having said that, businesses that fail to provide scenarios at a micro-level of conversion ultimately ignore the majority of their customers—those who sort of know what they want and those who are browsing or at the earliest stages in their buying decision process. Attention to micro-conversion scenarios also allows you to streamline your management through analytics by helping you to identify weaknesses in your overall persuasive system.

The purpose of a persuasion scenario is not necessarily to close the deal—the persuasive dimensions of many scenarios are satisfied if the goal of that scenario takes place.

CHAPTER TWENTY-SIX

Storyboarding and Prototyping the Scenarios

S toryboarding and prototyping involve the implementation and execution of our persuasive blueprint. They allow us to take our uncovery and wireframing to the next logical step. The majority of projects necessarily require the greatest amount of time, effort, and resources in this phase.

For the most part, implementing and executing persuasion entities for a Persuasion Architecture system is almost identical to creating persuasion entities for a typical marketing campaign with a few distinct differences.

The most important distinction is that *in a Persuasion Architecture project, each persuasion entity has a clear and distinct responsibility specified in the wireframe.* Evaluating the "creative" becomes a much more objective exercise as you measure everything you create against the intentions you developed in your plan. Does this Web page for personas A, B, and F answer the questions A, B, and F will ask? Does this TV ad stay true to its responsibility in this persona's scenario?

Persuasion Architecture eliminates most of the subjective bickering and pushback that usually happens during a typical implementation, since every persuasive entity is clearly mapped with goals and actions for each persona. The wireframe itself becomes the unifying standard for approval, in contrast to the more common practice of responding to the subjective opinions of the implementation team.

As the wireframe is implemented, you'll often find creative tensions rising from conflicting needs, from a persuasion entity that must address more than one persona, to various equally valid ideas of how to meet the business objective of that persuasion entity, to the inevitable politics involved in any significant project requiring more than one person to make a decision. These need to be reconciled and prioritized based on your business needs, the particular sensitivities of your personas, and whether these entities are critical paths for any personas.

We conceived Persuasion Architecture not simply as a process for developing persuasive systems, but also as a project management methodology. In our own practice, we've developed a software suite that allows us to track the disposition of every detail along the way and secure approval at every phase.

Almost all other marketing and persuasive efforts begin with storyboarding. In Persuasion Architecture you do not begin the "creative" until you know the parameters for what you need to create; it will provide a clear guide for what each persuasion entity must accomplish. For this reason, Persuasion Architecture smoothes the implementation phases.

Storyboarding basics

Uncovery, persona creation, and scenarios are all ways you plan strategy and determine objectives. The next step is to wireframe all those strategies to map out how you will achieve your goals. In the storyboard phase, you now move into tactics to execute that strategy.

Storyboarding is the process of making mock-ups of the visual presentation—creation proceeds iteratively through the approval process. It's where TV spots are written, billboards are laid out, and copy is written and rewritten. It's where your plan becomes a reality.

The process is exactly what it sounds like—imagine the pictures that are used in showing concepts when creating a film. In storyboarding, you are visualizing the vision, making it feel tangible and real. You experiment with the different elements that will help you reinforce the purpose of your persuasive system. You take your big-picture scenarios and wireframes and start focusing in on smaller picture details.

In a Persuasion Architecture project, the goal is not to be creative for the purpose of entertainment (although you certainly want your efforts to be engaging), but to be creative on-point, to maintain relevance at every step so that you meet the needs of the persona.

During storyboarding, you also decide which specific elements are necessary to your presentation: the copy, product pictures, color schemes, and dialog. This is your opportunity to consider elements individually and how they work in concert. You can test responses at the micro-level. You leave nothing to chance—the last thing you want is a soundtrack that brings to mind a funeral requiem when you're selling a hip, fast-paced product or service!

Until now, we've been discussing cognitive processes and choosing persuasion entities that were capable of maintaining the persuasive momentum. In storyboarding, the medium obviously makes a difference, and sometimes we discover that our vision can't be articulated through certain persuasion entities.

We can't go into an in-depth discussion here and offer advice for each medium—each has its body of expert practitioners who know best how to convey the messages we need to communicate. We strongly believe in turning to these resources for their valuable perspectives. We've covered many of the storyboarding elements associated with online persuasion in our books *Persuasive Online Copywriting* and *Call to Action*. For now, we can tell you color is immaterial if you are creating a radio spot, while the single cover image for a product brochure may take weeks to settle on.

Storyboarding clarifies exactly how we will implement the tactics that satisfy our business strategy so we can meet our business objectives. There will be multiple versions as people suggest improvements. At some point (fuzzier or clearer depending on the medium), a storyboard turns into a functional prototype that you hand off for implementation.

The prototype

In our Web-based practice, prototypes are essential to communicate to developers what we require from them. Handing your developer a series of checkout screens that look exactly as you want them to appear is more informative than simply providing a functional specification (saves time and money too!). The developer has only to figure out how to produce the desired functions.

For a sales letter, the prototype will be virtually identical to the actual letter that goes out, whereas the prototype for a television commercial may not actually involve film at all, but rather storyboards and scripts that are delivered for production.

The prototype and the eventual prototype freeze clarify exactly what you want implemented. There's little opportunity for misinterpretation once you've done the necessary planning. With prototype complete, the project heads into development—whatever programming, filming, recording, or assembly the persuasion entity requires. When the final product is fully functioning, it's launched.

And then the fun begins!

CHAPTER TWENTY-SEVEN

Accountable Marketing

Testing without understanding why you are testing is usually worthless. Scientists don't sit around coming up with a list of all the possible tests they could conduct. They start with a theory:

- "This drug causes a cellular reaction that reduces cholesterol."
- "This gene in your DNA controls protein production."

They then carefully devise specific tests that will prove or disprove their theories. If something doesn't happen as they predicted, they go back and reexamine their assumptions, revise the hypothesis, then test again.

Persuasion is not a numbers game! If it were, then some salespeople wouldn't out-produce other salespeople so dramatically. More accomplished salespeople have a better handle on the most important variables.

Persuasion is a skill, and that skill can be refined. In Persuasion Architecture, we make hypotheses based on everything we've learned, and then we test those hypotheses. The effects of persuasion can be tested and optimized. How?

You'll recall that every persuasion entity is created with our three important questions in mind:

1. What is the action we want someone to take?

2. Who are we trying to persuade to take the action?

3. What does that person need in order to feel confident taking that action?

And every persuasion entity is assigned a responsibility. It has a function to perform. It has to move personas forward through the persuasive system. In optimizing, we are looking for the places where persuasive momentum breaks down.

We've created a plan—the wireframe—in which we have control over what elements are created, why we created them, and how we created them. Essentially, this sets up the framework for a controlled experiment with hypotheses about how people will respond to the stimuli we present to them.

As marketers, we are trying to anticipate those elements we cannot control. Marketing deals with human beings, therefore it's a chaotic system. Persuasion Architecture is as close as you can come to a scientific experiment in marketing.

Optimize intelligently

In Persuasion Architecture, our goal is to limit the ratio of signal to noise so we can focus on the metrics that matter by tracking scenarios with key performance indicators that are clearly defined and by associating each scenario with its expected opportunity. In other words, we set up our experiments so we can track all the micro-actions to see how they influence the macro-actions we want our customers to take. Clearly defining goals upfront is crucial to setting up and measuring these scenarios.

Depending on your business and the business intelligence you have available, you can determine the expected revenue each persuasion scenario will drive. If your early-in-the-buying-decision-process scenarios aren't working well, you can expect those scenarios that occur later in the buying decision process to generate less revenue.

Take our Susan profile from Chapter Twenty-Five. If she finds it easier to identify the television she wants through one of your competitors, it is unlikely that she'll purchase a television from you—making it that much less likely that you'll be her first choice when she's ready to buy her home theater system.

How much revenue the Susan persona can generate is dependent on the size of your market, your competitive position, the strength of your brand, and the persuasive momentum you build into your persuasive system.

We need to create a "dashboard" that allows us to see the most important business data. It should also give us a way to determine whether our scenarios are performing as planned, and to describe the nature of the opportunity gap between what we planned and what we observed. This lets us focus our energies when we optimize. If, for example, Susan is critical to your business and represents a large market opportunity, optimizing her scenario would have priority over a less-critical scenario.

Testing and measuring scenarios allows us to resolve conflicts. Conflicts may occur when we've given preference to one persona over another in overlapping persuasion entities. Certainly there are times we need to evaluate decisions made in storyboarding—when we test and measure carefully, we can evaluate the results of changes we make to those entities, always mindful that we don't want to sacrifice the benefit of a larger opportunity to a smaller one.

The measurement of marketing ROI

A recent *Harvard Business Review* article reveals some sorry numbers. A survey of five hundred businesses shows an average return on investment of 4 percent. Ouch! Another study shows doubling the ad spend only resulted in an average 1 to 2 percent sales increase. According to the article: "Marketers aren't unhappy because they can't measure marketing performance. They're unhappy because they now can—and they don't like what they see."[1]

These days, it's possible to measure discrete components. But because these components are part of a much larger system, *marketers can only measure a return based on either the tactic or the overall result.* They can't measure the effect within the system.

A new client had recently discontinued a pay-per-click campaign because, based on their Web analytics, the customers who arrived on the Web site via that campaign were not converting into sales. The return on investment for the tactic itself didn't seem to pan out as expected. Ditching the ad seemed a wise thing to do. If the effort doesn't yield a return, don't bother throwing more money at it.

When the client discontinued the pay-per-click, their advertising expenses went down. So did the overall conversions for their Web site and overall sales. Turns out, that advertisement *did* work. The targeted keyword was very effective in attracting customers early in their buying process—customers arrived prepared to gather information, not to buy. The ad simply worked within a different time horizon and a different part of the persuasive system. An inability to tie these two concepts together within the system prompted the client to make a decision.

A Six Sigma perspective

Anything that results in a lower level of customer satisfaction or a lost customer constitutes a defect, a flaw, in the sales process.

When your persuasive momentum breaks down and a customer fails to complete the scenario, your persuasive system may have a service defect. Your process may not have delivered on your promise; at some point, your customer may have stopped perceiving you as relevant to their needs. At least, that's how you would evaluate things if you adopted a Six Sigma perspective (which Persuasion Architecture does).

W. Edwards Deming, considered by many the Father of the Quality Revolution, believed if individuals can't interact with a system successfully, the problem lies not in the people using the system, but in the system itself. He also said, "If you can't describe what you are doing as a process, you don't know what you're doing."[2] We couldn't agree more!

If you think you can't achieve a framework for prediction, it means you probably don't understand the system. Just as persuasive systems are more complex so are return-on-investment calculations. Proper definitions are essential.

Six Sigma defined

Six Sigma is a disciplined, data-driven approach and methodology that eliminates defects in any process (driving toward six standard deviations between the mean and the nearest specification limit). Six Sigma has been applied in areas that range from manufacturing to transactional businesses, products to services. The goal is to eliminate waste by achieving near-perfect results.

Many companies have incorporated Six Sigma "not just as a tool for operational efficiency, but as an enterprise-wide business strategy with direct bottom line impact . . . Six Sigma has been indisputably successful in eliminating waste, reducing variance and increasing productivity and profits."[3] General Electric, AlliedSignal, and other well-known manufacturers credit Six Sigma with having produced billions of dollars in efficiencies.

Six Sigma's value is not limited to manufacturers, although there are some areas, such as advertising, in which application is difficult if not impossible. Organizations use it to optimize such non-manufacturing processes as accounts receivable, sales, and research and development.

The fundamental objective of a Six Sigma methodology is to implement a measurement-based strategy that focuses on process-enhancement and variation-reduction in an application. This is accomplished through the use of two Six Sigma sub-methodologies: Define, Measure, Analyze, Improve, Control (DMAIC); and Define, Measure, Analyze, Design, Verify (DMADV). DMAIC is a way to look for incremental improvement in existing processes that are falling below specification. DMADV is a way to develop new processes or products at Six Sigma quality levels. It can also be used when a process needs more than incremental improvement.

Six Sigma in action

It's easier to understand and apply Six Sigma to a manufacturing system—you can see the process; it's tangible. There are marketers who try to apply Six Sigma to their activities, but unlike manufacturing, marketing consists of many intangibles. And it's the rare marketer who has systematized her activities in a way that lends itself to Six Sigma analysis.

Because Persuasion Architecture offers a more holistic description for the entire system, it allows us to identify the component parts of the system that need measuring and improving. You can identify and measure specific service and process defects, then ask, "Why are they happening?" The answer to that question may uncover underlying reasons for customer dissatisfaction and defection. We often find there's more than one reason or root cause contributing to a service defect.

Once you've identified the chief contributors—copywriting, usability, visual communications, and marketing plan assumptions—you can refine the persuasive system to better serve the customer. For example, at a macro-level you may define the problem as an inability to convert sufficient prospects to leads. You would want to measure your conversions to leads, analyze any causal factors (a.k.a. chief contributors), and improve those variables against a control. Then, repeat the process continually until you are satisfied the results are optimal.

At a micro-level, you may define the problem as a high rejection rate (customers exiting the Web site) on a home page. First, you would want to measure and define a baseline. Then, you could use surveys, click-through pathing, content analysis, sales process analysis, Persuasion Architecture scenario analysis, time on page, and other data to determine root causes.

Analyzing the results will help you determine what needs to be improved so you can fix the leading root causes (e.g., copy, design, navigation, interaction). Test the leading variables to see what changes make the biggest impact. Then maintain the variable (e.g., fresh content) to control the improvement. Then repeat the process continually until you are satisfied the results are optimal. It may sound like pure theory, but Six Sigma is practical and yields enormous return on investment.

We use both sub-methodologies. Persuasive system design as embodied in Persuasion Architecture is similar to DMADV. DMAIC better applies to systems that are not designed through Persuasion Architecture, but are using Persuasion Architecture to optimize implicit scenarios. This cognate helps us tie other business metrics to Kaizen, the Japanese philosophy of continuous improvement.

Applying Six Sigma to persuasive systems makes everything measurable. The result is a repeatable process.

A system for prioritizing

The need to move beyond simple metrics-tracking to manipulate and improve numbers is obvious. Six Sigma and other methodologies focus on not only measuring marketing activities, but also understanding variables that affect metrics, and controlling and influencing the ones with the greatest effect on the bottom line. These are "levers."

Six Sigma provides a framework to determine and prioritize what's mission-critical. Underlying the approach is a structure that uses measurements before, during, and after development. Six Sigma works for any area that can impact a customer's perception of quality. *Most failures in getting a customer to convert (to a sale, lead, subscription, registration, etc.) stem from a perceived lack of value, trust, confidence, security, or relevance.*

Six Sigma is an ideal. The term literally means 3.4 or fewer errors per million opportunities (99.9997 percent accuracy). You're probably gasping, "That's not possible. I can't apply that to marketing! I'll never sell *everyone!*" But don't get caught up in the number; it's not representative of the complete methodology. It's like a glass being half full or half empty.

To achieve outstanding results, we need to look at things from the other side. What happened to those who did not complete their scenarios? Perhaps they were not yet ready to buy, intend to return, or are still researching. Perhaps they were disappointed or dissatisfied. Incomplete scenarios represent potential defects in the system.

Six Sigma drives sustained improvement in productivity, customer satisfaction, and loyalty to reduce cost and increase marketing spend efficiency. When using a methodical, disciplined approach such as Six Sigma, you face the creative tensions you need to overcome. You can't subjectively quantify how persuasive your content or imagery is. What you say, how you say it, and how well you address the information customers seek will all be critical to meeting customer needs and driving conversion.

CHAPTER TWENTY-EIGHT

Persuasion Architecture: A Six-Step Process

Persuasion Architecture is the discipline we created to address the needs of both businesses and customers in an emerging media landscape that establishes a new experience economy. Throughout this book, we have explained the principles that inform Persuasion Architecture. These principles aren't new; they've been around, in one form or another, for as long as people have been trying to figure out the most effective ways to exchange this for that. Technology may rearrange the furniture, but the same people still live there.

Persuasion Architecture is a methodology for implementing the planning, design, development, and optimization of your persuasion entities. This systematic approach insures you start with a solid foundation that persuades your customers more effectively and allows you to measure activity so you can manage your persuasion entities more intelligently.

We have developed integrated software applications that manage project complexity. These software tools are structured in such a way to accommodate a variety of persuasion entities, which allows you to unify and integrate your persuasive efforts across your multi-channel activities.

Our methodology evolved specifically from our own online applications and continues to evolve as we work with clients architecting increasingly complex persuasive systems that interconnect with other persuasive entities across a variety of media.

Let's take some time to recap the strands of Persuasion Architecture's methodology so we can review how all these persuasive efforts fit together.

The phases of Persuasion Architecture

Persuasion Architecture has six phases: The process begins with Uncovery, continues with Wireframing, Storyboarding, and Prototyping, then enters the actual production phase in Development. The final phase, Optimization, provides for ongoing testing and measuring to ensure that management decisions are always based on solid information.

Now that we've explained the whole process in detail, let's step back and take in the big picture.

1. Uncovery. Uncovery provides a foundation, without which any attempt at persuasion crumbles. The goals of uncovery are to identify the value of the business and articulate it in a way that matters to the customer, so you can create the best merger between selling and buying for your situation. Toward the end of the uncovery process, you start creating personas that give insight into the customers' buying processes and help you understand each customer's individual needs, wants, and desires through detailed narratives.

Uncovery is the only piece in Persuasion Architecture that can stand alone. You can turn directly to optimizing an existing scenario once you have completed uncovery. But no other step in Persuasion Architecture can take place in the absence of uncovery.

2. Wireframing. Persuasion Architecture's wireframing defines the "what" of the creative process, providing the structure that will deliver the persuasive experience. It ensures the maintenance of persuasive momentum by keeping things relevant, cognitive process to cognitive process.

3. Storyboarding. Storyboarding iteratively creates the mock-ups in which you flesh out the structure of the wireframe, designing the different elements that will help you reinforce the purpose of your persuasive system. Experts in the medium for which the persuasive entity is designed help refine what is appropriate in addressing the needs of the persona and the scenario in the context of the medium.

4. Prototyping. The storyboard is frozen, and the prototype is virtually indistinguishable from the final product. Because the prototype is exhaustively specific, completing your project will consume fewer resources—it gets done correctly the first time.

5. Development. The goal of development is to produce everything that was specified in the prototype.

6. Optimization. Your finished product offers a meaningful starting point for testing and measuring. Ongoing optimization requires monitoring your metrics to evaluate the effectiveness of the scenarios you defined during wireframing. Testing and measuring in order to optimize is the only way you come full circle in Persuasion Architecture—the only way you can determine how closely you are meeting your objectives and how you can improve your results.

A system for continuous improvement

Because Persuasion Architecture is a meticulously planned process, the attention to detail allows the persuasive system to become self-identifying. During uncovery, we explore objectives and assumptions. During wireframing, we are creating the strategy that will allow us to reach our objectives. During storyboarding and prototyping, we are planning the tactics to implement our strategy, and during development, we are executing.

Once we actually experience how customers interact with the system, we can go back to revisit anything from the underlying assumptions to the actual tactics—they all are connected to each other within this process.

Prospective clients early in the buying cycle for our services often ask us, "How do we know this will work?" and "How do we know we'll be collecting the right data and making the right assumptions?" It's the process that works; it's only partially reliant on our talent. If a business can commit to being a part of this process, it will work. And if we've made mistakes, as everyone inevitably does, we'll know exactly where they are. The mistakes are always self-identifying.

When clients understand the Persuasion Architecture methodology, they are much more confident about proceeding. After all, it's an intuitively sound process. It has to work. By the time uncovery concludes with the creation of personas, those who entered into the process with trepidation are complete believers. We suspect that's because very few people have ever given this much thought to their persuasive systems before.

Celebrating Your Cats' Meows

The day is short, the work is much, the laborers are slothful. It is not incumbent upon you to finish the job, however, neither are you free from doing all you can to complete it.[1]

—Rabbi Tarfon, *Ethics of the Fathers*

As marketers in today's landscape, we must walk a different path. No longer will our product-centered, mass-market habits serve us well. The interconnectedness of emerging media means we must focus on the customer and create persuasive systems that have at their core an understanding of human motivations. The unfolding experience economy makes this demand on all of us.

The experience we must strive for is no longer about what we promise. It is entirely about what we deliver. The goal of satisfying our business objectives requires us to model interactivity within and across our persuasive systems so we can meet the needs of our customers. To accomplish this, we must understand why our customers do things and how they go about doing them. To sell well, we must embrace a willingness to sell small.

In this book, we have dredged up many questions that still remain unanswered. Anticipation of what is yet to come, what we have yet to discover, is part of the journey's excitement. We will all continue to learn.

Persuasion Architecture will "do no harm"

We have presented Persuasion Architecture as a set of big principles. In fact there's a lot of detail we simply couldn't put in this book. If you are thinking, *This is a big undertaking*, you're right. It is. But then, nothing worthwhile is ever without effort.

The good news is Persuasion Architecture is a methodology that, even when applied in smaller, less-than-ideal pieces, will still improve any persuasive system. Tackling these principles one at a time is a reasonable way to start.

So we urge you: please, *do try this at home*. The only wrong response to this book is no response at all.

How to apply Persuasion Architecture to an already great campaign

Holly Buchanan, one of our Persuasion Architects, offered a real-world example from Logitech in her blog, *Marketing to Women Online*.[2]

Logitech did so many things right when they put together a brilliant marketing campaign for their video-calling product, Quick Cam. Marketers often assume men are the only business travelers. But Logitech obviously did some uncovery and found out that women travel for business just as often as men do. They decided to target a female executive who has a deep desire to stay connected with her husband and children while she's on the road. The persona may be female, but this is also a moving message that can connect with travelers irrespective of gender.

Logitech creates a driving point for their traveling female executive: a TV commercial where she's able to say goodnight to her family using video calling. Copy in the commercial includes "make a better connection" and "video calling made easy"—trigger phrases that appeal to this persona. The end of the commercial directs viewers to the Web site.

Our engaged viewer continues to the funnel point of this scenario: Logitech's home page. She discovers an element on the home page that shows a screen shot from a video calling commercial. It's not the commercial she saw, but it includes the same language from the ad: "Video Calling Made Easy." Logitech provided just enough continuity to connect the TV commercial to the Web site's home page. Good job!

But here the scenario starts to break down. Our viewer's first call to action is: "Current TV Commercials." Let's assume this is an important link to her (that she doesn't actually want to get directly to the product). If she clicks on the link, she lands on a page with the traveling mom commercial. She's reassured she's in the right place and on her way to the right product. That's good.

But where can she go from here? There's no obvious call to action. The persuasive momentum grinds to a halt. She seems to be at a dead end. She can watch other commercials, but that's a distraction. Only if she scrolls *all the way down* to the bottom of a page will she discover a weak call to action: a graphic checkmark with a "More Information" link.

Had Logitech taken the time to think through this scenario in advance, they could have anticipated the problem here. The questions they needed to ask were easy: "Where does she want to go next? What questions is she asking at this point? What is the action we want her take?" The answers would help them provide an appropriate call to action—say, "See how easy it is to use"—right next to the commercial image, right where her eyes were focused. A link like this isn't a dead end; it sustains persuasive momentum.

Logitech could then add a link to the product page, based on the questions our viewer would ask there: "Does it come with a set of two cameras? Or do I need to buy two? In all the examples of video calling, there are two cameras—are they sold separately or as a set?" Once again, a link would provide persuasive momentum and give the customer confidence to enter into the conversion funnel, whether that funnel is online or at a local store.

A lot of work and thought went into Logitech's commercial. If they had taken the time to fix the online details, they would have a very persuasive scenario.

This is a simple example of Persuasion Architecture's power to create, analyze, and optimize persuasive systems. You can—and should—apply it to almost any marketing effort to dramatically improve your results.

Get started

Start with uncovery. If you simply do uncovery, you'll learn a lot. Then start thinking about personas—what they would find relevant, how they will approach you, what they need from you. Even if you simply toss around persona ideas, you will benefit. Then plan a small, simple scenario—a pay-per-click, a television ad, an e-mail. Flesh it out. Execute it. Evaluate it. Then go forward from there.

Finishing, having a perfect persuasive system, isn't as important as having *something*.

Incorporate these ideas into your tool kit—you won't regret it. Bell-ringing still works. Not as well, but it's still working. After all, cats will agree to conditioning when it suits them.

However, we can imagine the day when someone's skill set is reduced to simply ringing that one bell. And the cat will eventually wander off in search of something more interesting.

Imagine yourself in a vast concert hall, about to conduct a performance. Before you stands a solitary bell-ringer with one bell in his hand. Through that bell alone, can you offer your audience the experience they came to hear?

Now, surround your bell-ringer with percussion that creates a pulse of momentum, woodwinds that sparkle with interest and individuality, strings that pull at emotions, brass that punctuates and heralds. Imagine filling your vast concert hall with a rich, complicated, beautiful sound that will captivate your audience. Imagine giving your audience exactly what they want to hear.

We promise. *That's* the way to keep your customers meowing for more!

NOTES

Introduction

1. Persuasion Architecture™ is a trademark belonging to Future Now, Inc. The inventors are Bryan Eisenberg, Jeffrey Eisenberg, and John Quarto-vonTivadar.

Chapter One: Dogs, Cats, and Marketing

1. The bell part may be apocryphal. "It is popularly believed that Pavlov always signaled the occurrence of food by ringing a bell. In fact his writings record the use of a wide variety of auditory stimuli including whistles, metronomes, tuning forks and the bubbling of air through water, in addition to a range of visual stimuli. When, in the 1990s, it became easier for Western scientists to visit Pavlov's laboratory in Moscow, no trace of a bell could be found," *Wikipedia,* s.v. "Ivan Pavlov," http://en.wikipedia.org/wiki/Ivan_Pavlov (accessed January 16, 2006).

2. From the perspective of the pooch, there is nothing inherently suggestive about ringing a bell. With your average, unconditioned dog, you can ring a bell until your arm drops off —he's simply not going to salivate. Only when you repeatedly associate the sound of the bell with the immediate appearance of something tasty does the bell-food relationship begin to form.

3. Evolving from the idea of classic conditioning, "operant conditioning" involves the modification of responses based on the consequences of the behavior: desired behavior is rewarded (which strengthens the response), undesired behavior is punished (which weakens the response).

4. *Wikipedia,* s.v. "John B. Watson," http://en.wikipedia.org/wiki/John_B._Watson (accessed January 16, 2006).

5. *Wikipedia,* s.v. "Little Albert Experiment," http://en.wikipedia.org/wiki/Little_Albert_experiment (accessed January 16, 2006).

6. Dr. Robert Kentridge. "Trial and Error, from the Rise of Thorndike to the Fall of J.B. Watson," 1995. http://www.dur.ac.uk/robert.kentridge/comp6.html (accessed February 5, 2006).

7. Chris Locke. "A brief look at the strangely entangled history of psychology, advertising and public relations" *Chief Blogging Officer* (February 4, 2005). http://www.chiefbloggingofficer.com/2005/02/brief-look-at-strangely-entangled.html (accessed January 16, 2006).

8. James T. Todd (Eastern Michigan University). "Behavior Analysis Association of Michigan: Behavior Analysis Q & A," Behavior Analysis Association of Michigan (November 15, 2005). http://www.baam.emich.edu/BAAMMainpages/BAAMfaq.htm (accessed January 16, 2006).

9. Ibid. "The issue really isn't whether dog or cats are [different in intelligence], but the range and type of reinforcers cats and dogs are sensitive to. Dogs are highly social pack animals. Their behavior can be strongly reinforced by just a little attention from other members of their pack, especially the pack leader (you). Thus, there are many opportunities for a dog's behavior to be shaped by incidental, attention-based reinforcement . . . Cats generally are less social and less sensitive to attention as a potential reinforcer. Their behavior is less likely to be shaped by incidental attention. Unlike dogs, which are

hunter/scavengers and will consume a very wide range of foods at almost any time, cats consume a narrower range of foods and will often do so only at specific times."

10. Pat Welch. "Catku: What Is the Sound of One Cat Napping," Andrews McMeel Publishing, 2004. 5, 27, 13. These selections were excerpted from a circulating e-mail that landed in Lisa's inbox. Via communications like this one, Lisa has also learned that any number of dogs will happily change light bulbs for their master or mistress while the correct answer to "How many cats does it take to change a light bulb?" is "Cats do not change light bulbs. People change light bulbs." So the real question is: "How long will it be before I can expect some light and some dinner?"

11. Lisa Gubernick. "Beyond ballyhoo," *Forbes* (September 23, 1985). http://www.highbeam.com/library/docRef.asp?docid=1G1:3946430&refid=blog_2030486&openRef=1, (accessed January 16, 2006).

Chapter Two: Experiencing the Brand

1. Within the realm of self-actualization, Maslow identified seventeen meta-needs, or "being values" (B-values), which describe the various needs people seek to fulfill in the process of self-actualization. Meta-needs fuel the process of self-actualization. Unlike deficit needs, meta-needs are not hierarchical—individuals prioritize and choose the values that matter most to them. Maslow identified these meta-needs: Truth, Goodness, Beauty, Wholeness, Transcendence, Aliveness, Uniqueness, Perfection, Necessity, Completion, Justice, Order, Simplicity, Richness, Effortlessness, Playfulness, and Self-Sufficiency.

2. *About.com,* s.v. "Introduction to Pop, Part I: The History of Pop Timeline" (by Mary Bellis, September 1999). http://inventors.about.com/library/weekly/aa091699.htm, (accessed January 17, 2006).

3. *BuzzMachine,* s.v. "Dear Mr. Dell," (by Jeff Jarvis, August 17, 2005). http://www.buzzmachine.com/index.php/2005/08/17/dear-mr-dell, (accessed January 17, 2006).

4. *CNNMoney.com,* s.v. "Coke slaps on a new tagline 'Welcome to the Coke side of life' to mark beverage giant's new aggressive marketing push in 2006," (by Parija Bhatnagar, December 8, 2005). http://money.cnn.com/2005/12/08/news/fortune500/coke_meeting/index.htm, (accessed January 17, 2006).

5. *AFA Journal.org,* s.v. "Media consumption underestimated," (American Families Association, May 2004). http://www.afajournal.org/2004/may/504noi.asp, (accessed January 17, 2006).

6. Personal communication from Jeff Einstein.

7. In his book, *On Bullshit* (Princeton University Press, January 10, 2005), Harry G. Frankfurt, Professor of Philosophy Emeritus at Princeton University, discusses the growing postmodern cultural experience of creating images and impressions with little concern for their ties to truth.

Chapter Three: Friction and Customer Experience

1. Diane Brady. "How the net can find markets for the obscure," *Business Week* (December 19, 2005), 78. "Long tail" is a term coined by Chris Anderson, Editor-in-Chief of *Wired*, referring to the bell-curve tail on the demand curve.

2. Ibid.

Chapter Four: Why Marketing Is Simple But Hard

1. *Thoemmes Continuum: The History of Ideas,* s.v. "Marketing," (Morgan Witzel, 2000). http://www.thoemmes.com/economics/marketing_intro.htm (accessed January 17, 2006).

2. If you are looking for information about these stories, General Electric and 3M offer notable examples in the realm of production and performance. The logistics stories behind businesses like Dell and Wal-Mart are well understood, as are the finance stories behind companies like Drexel Burnham Lambert (now defunct), Goldman-Sachs, and Citibank.

3. Frederick F. Reichheld. "The Loyalty Effect: the satisfaction trap," *Essays on the relationship between loyalty and profits.* (Essay #5, 1995). http://www.loyaltyrules.com/bainweb/pdfs/cms/marketing/22.pdf, (accessed January 17, 2006).

4. Ibid.

5. Steve Greenhouse. "How Costco became the anti-Wal-Mart." *The New York Times* (July 17, 2005). http://www.nytimes.com/2005/07/17/business/yourmoney/17costco.html?ex=1279252800&en=8b31033c5b6a6d68&ei=5088&partner=rssnyt&emc=rss, (accessed January 17, 2006).

6. Stanley Holmes and Wendy Zellner. "The Costco Way: Higher wages mean higher profits. But try telling Wall Street," *Business Week* (April 4, 2004). http://www.businessweek.com/magazine/content/04_15/b3878084_mz021.htm (accessed February 5, 2006).

7. Robert Hutchins Goddard is considered the pioneer of modern rocketry and the man for whom the Goddard Space Flight Center was named in 1959. "Though his work in the field was revolutionary, he was often ridiculed for his theories, which were ahead of their time. He received little recognition during his own lifetime, but would eventually come to be called the 'father of modern rocketry' for his life's work." *Wikipedia,* s.v. "Robert Goddard." http://en.wikipedia.org/wiki/Robert_Hutchins_Goddard, (accessed January 17, 2006).

Chapter Five: Marketers Out of Control

1. *George Silverman's Word-of-Mouth Marketing Blog.* "Disturbing memo to marketers" (August 12, 2005). http://wordofmouth.typepad.com/george_silvermans_word_of/2005/08/disturbing_memo.html (accessed January 17, 2006).

2. "ANA 2000 Annual Conference Provides Powerful Insights on Brand Building in the New E-conomy," (October 16, 2000). http://www.ana.net/news/2000/10_16_00.cfm, (accessed January 17, 2006).

3. Personal communication from Mark Huffman, January 4, 2006.

4. "TiVo is reportedly working with some of the biggest ad agencies around to create DVR-based advertising search. That would enable TiVo subscribers to run searches for ads that are important to them at a time that is convenient for them. Imagine, giving consumers power in when they view an advertisement instead of hitting them over the head while they're trying to enjoy Arrested Development (when it's on)." "TiVo + ad search = :)" (by Chris Thilk, November 28, 2005). http://www.adjab.com/2005/11/28/tivo-ad-search, (accessed January 17, 2006).

5. eMarketer. "B-C Online Customer Acquisition," (November 5, 2005).

6. eMarketer. "Online Consumer Selling: A Multi-Channel Perspective US Consumers' Most Common Starting Point for the Online Shopping Process," (February 2005).

7. Forrester Research. "Learning the Value of Effective Site Design: Why Most Firms Don't Measure Design's Value—And How They Must Change," (December 2005).

8. ANA News Press Release. op cit.

Chapter Seven: How Customers Buy

1. For those too young to remember, the Yellow Pages is a thick book filled with phone numbers and cheesy ads that early man used to find local business solutions.

2. For want of a nail, the shoe was lost,
   For want of the shoe, the horse was lost,
   For want of the horse, the rider was lost,
   For want of the rider, the battle was lost,
   For want of the battle, the kingdom was lost,
   And all for the want of a horseshoe nail!
   Benjamin Franklin. *The Complete Poor Richard Almanac, 1758,* (Facsimile edition, Vol. 2: 1970), 375.
3. Bryan Eisenberg. ROI Marketing. "The New Frontier: Complex Sales," *ClickZ* (January 30, 2004). http://www.clickz.com/experts/crm/traffic/article.php/3305521, (accessed January 17, 2006).

Chapter Eleven: A Web of Interactivity

1. *Future Now: A Day in the Life of a Persuasion Architect,* s.v. "Finding a gift that makes sense" (by Joshua Hay, December 8, 2005). http://persuasion.typepad.com/architect/2005/12/finding_a_gift_.html, (accessed January 17, 2006).
2. Chris Gaither and Meg James. "Web Pulls Ad Buyers from TV," *Los Angeles Times* (May 18, 2005) C1.
3. *Doubleclick.com.* "DoubleClick's Touchpoints III: The Internet's Role in the Modern Purchase Process," (July 2005) 3. http://www.doubleclick.com/us/knowledge_central/trend_reports/ad_serving/default.asp, (accessed January 17, 2005).
4. Roy H. Williams. *Secret Formulas of the Wizard of Ads,* (Austin, TX: Bard Press, 1999) 50.

Chapter Twelve: Brands Cross Channels

1. *ClickZ,* s.v. "Multichannel marketing: channibalism?" (by Jack Aaronson, CRM Strategies, May 15, 2003). http://www.clickz.com/experts/crm/crm_strat/article.php/2205571, (accessed January 17, 2006).
2. *DoubleClick,* s.v. "Multi-channel shopping study—holiday 2003," (January 2004). http://www.doubleclick.com/us/knowledge_central/documents/RESEARCH/dc_multichannel_holiday_0401.pdf, (accessed January 17, 2006).
3. *ClickZ,* s.v. "Think like a multichannel company" (by Jack Aaronson, CRM Strategies, February 19, 2004). http://www.clickz.com/experts/crm/crm_strat/article.php/3314681, (accessed January 17, 2006). Used with permission.
4. Ibid.

Chapter Thirteen: Insights and Customer Data

1. The Perception Analyzer (PA) is MSInteractive's dial technology feedback tool that makes it possible to elicit instant, honest, and unbiased feedback from a group through the use of wireless hand-held dials. http://www.perceptionanalyzer.com, (accessed February 4, 2006).

Chapter Fourteen: Personalization or "Persona-lization"

1. *Internet Retailer,* s.v. "Shoppers want personalized web content, but not personal data disclosure," (August 18, 2005). http://Internetretailer.com/dailyNews.asp?id=15848, (accessed January 17, 2006).
2. Ibid.

Chapter Fifteen: Introducing Personas

1. *The American Heritage Dictionary of the English Language.* Fourth Edition (New York: Houghton Mifflin Company, 2000).

2. David Keirsey. *Please Understand Me II: Temperament, Character, Intelligence* (Prometheus Nemesis Book Company, 1998). www.keirsey.com, (accessed February 4, 2006).

3. Kris Oser. "The sisomo of Kevin Roberts at Ad:Tech: Saatchi & Saatchi CEO as New Age Guru," *AdAge.com Interactive News*, (November 8, 2005).http://www.adage.com/news.cms? newsId=46616#, (accessed January 17, 2006).

4. Ibid.

5. *The Origin of Brands Blog*, s.v. "Nobody wants to be like Mr. Six," (by Laura Ries, July 26, 2004). http://ries.typepad.com/ries_blog/2004/07/nobody_wants_to.htm, (accessed January 17, 2006).

6. *ClickZ*, s.v. "Nothing Serious, We're Only Engaged," (by Rebecca Lieb, Smarter Marketing. November 11, 2005). http://www.clickz.com/experts/brand/buzz/article.php/ 3563376, (accessed January 17, 2006).

7. *AdAge.com*, s.v. "Gap's celebrity-endorser marketing strategy bombs: as sales slump continues, retailer pulls back on glitzy tv ads," (by Mya Frazier, November 28, 2005). http://adage.com/news.cms?newsId=46924, (accessed January 17, 2006).

8. Rebecca Lieb. op cit.

9. Rebecca Lieb. op cit.

10. *GrokDotCom*, s.v. "The power of emotion" (January 15, 2002). http:// www.grokdotcom.com/powerofemotion.htm, (accessed January 17, 2006).

Chapter Sixteen: Uncovering the Knowable

1. The concept of uncovery isn't new to the business world. Many actually refer to the practice as "discovery." But there's a reason we don't use this word; in our minds it carries two counterproductive associations. In the world of law, discovery is that often-adversarial, tooth-pulling exercise in which opposing interests "share" information. Discovery also brings to mind an exercise in exploration, where the forces that write history discover something previously unknown to them. Certainly it must have surprised Native Americans to learn they had been discovered, when they knew all along that they already existed. In this sense, discovery is a one-way road upon which walk the self-important.

Chapter Seventeen: Disclosing the Necessary

1. *J.D. Power and Associates Reports*, s.v. "Automotive Web Site Traffic Still Strong; Manufacturer and Dealership Sites Attract More Buyers" (October 10, 2002). http://www.jdpa.com/ presspass/pr/pressrelease.asp?ID=2002107, (accessed January 17, 2006).

2. A study by Feedback Research, a division of Claria Corp, "uncovered that 63 percent of consumers [who said they use the Internet as an information source in their vehicle purchasing decisions] knew what type of vehicle they wanted to purchase and only considered that one type" while comparing different brands. Price, size of car, reputation of manufacturer, and design/style considerations were the most important factors to those researching an automotive purchase online. *Autoremarketing*, s.v. "Study: 58% use Internet to gather info and shop" (November 9, 2005). http://www.autoremarketing.com/ ar/news/story.html?id=4188, (accessed January 17, 2006).

3. Daniel Lyons. "Attack of the blogs," *Forbes* (November 2005).

Chapter Eighteen: Mapping Business Topology

1. Tim Berners-Lee with Mark Fischetti. *Weaving the Web: The Original Design and Ultimate Destiny of the World Wide Web by Its Inventor,* First Edition (San Francisco: Harper, 1999), 12.

2. Jim Collins. *Good to Great: Why Some Companies Make the Leap . . . and Others Don't* (New York: Harper Collins, 2001).

3. Melanie Warner and Stuart Elliott. "Frothier Than Ever: The Tall Cold One Bows to the Stylish One," *The New York Times* (August 15, 2005), C1.

Chapter Nineteen: The Topology of a Sale

1. Kevin Dugan. "The Considered Purchase," Strategic Public Relations blog (August 13, 2003). http://prblog.typepad.com/strategic_public_relation/2003/08/the_considered_.html, (accessed January 17, 2006).

2. *ClickZ,* s.v. "The New Frontier: Complex Sales" (Bryan Eisenberg, ROI Marketing, January 30, 2004). http://www.clickz.com/experts/crm/traffic/article.php/3305521, (accessed January 17, 2006).

3. Roy H. Williams. "Transactional and relational redux." *Monday Morning Memo* (February 10, 2003). http://www.wizardacademy.com/showmemo.asp?id=61, (accessed January 17, 2006).

Chapter Twenty: The Human Operating System

1. World POPClick Projection. US Census Bureau. http://www.census.gov/ipc/www/popclockworld.html, (accessed November 26, 2005 at 18:29 GMT).

2. Enjoyable reads for the lay person include *The Art of Speed Reading People: Harness the Power of Personality Type and Create What You Want in Business and Life* by Paul D. Tiegar and Barbara Barron-Tiegar (Little, Brown and Co., 1998) and *Please Understand Me II: Temperament, Character, Intelligence* by David Keirsey (Prometheus Nemesis Book Company, 1998).

3. For a discussion of the differences between Myers-Briggs' and David Keirsey's positions, see "Keirsey Temperament versus Myers-Briggs Types." http://users.viawest.net/~keirsey/difference.html, (accessed January 18, 2006).

4. In his "third cut," Keirsey examines Thinking and Feeling in relation to Sensing, and Judging and Perceiving in relation to Intuition, giving him twelve temperament types. Only in the last assignment of attributes does he address Extroversion and Introversion, creating the sixteen temperaments that reflect Myers-Briggs's sixteen temperament types.

Chapter Twenty-One: Choosing Personas

1. We chose the word *wireframing* deliberately, knowing it can be a loaded word. In terms of persuasion, wireframing is about framing the cognitive process. The cognitive process is the essence of a persuasive system, and how those cognitive processes are connected contextually is what we are defining in a wireframe.

2. *MarketingVox,* s.v. "User demographics, intent differ among search engines" (July 28, 2005). http://www.marketingvox.com/archives/2005/07/28/user_demographics_intent_differ_among_search_engines/ (accessed January 18, 2006).

Chapter Twenty-Two: Bringing Personas to Life

1. John Steinbeck. "2/13-14/1962 letter to Robert Wallsten," from *Steinbeck: A Life in Letters*, Elaine A. Steinbeck and Robert Wallsten, ed. (New York:Viking Penguin, 1975).

2. *Permanente Journal,* s.v. "CPC Corner: An overview of empathy" (James T. Hardee, MD, November 2003, Vol. 7 No. 4). http://xnet.kp.org/permanentejournal/fall03/cpc.html, (accessed January 18, 2006).

3. David S. Freeman. "Beyond Structure: LA's and NY's most popular screenwriting, development and fiction workshop." http://www2.beyondstructure.com/start.php, (accessed January 18, 2006).

4. Gary McWilliams. "Minding the store: analyzing customers, Best Buy decides not all are welcome," *The Wall Street Journal* (November 8, 2004) A1. Copyright 2004 by Dow Jones & Co., Inc. Reproduced with permission of Dow Jones & Co., Inc. via Copyright Clearance Center.

5. Ibid.

Chapter Twenty-Three: The Architecture Metaphor

1. Frank Lloyd Wright. "In the Cause of Architecture," *Architectural Record* (March 1908). Reprinted in *Frank Lloyd Wright Collected Writings 1939-1949*, Vol. 1 (New York: Rizzoli, 1994), 87–88.

Chapter Twenty-Four: Wireframing As an Interactivity Map

1. This term should not be confused with the standard Web design term for *wireframing*, which constitutes a layout of site elements on a page.

Chapter Twenty-Seven: Accountable Marketing

1. Kevin J. Clancy and Randy L. Stone. "Don't blame the metrics," *Harvard Business Review* (June 1, 2005).

2. *BrainyQuote*, s.v. "W. Edwards Deming." http://www.brainyquote.com/quotes/authors/w/w_edwards_deming.html, (accessed February 3, 2006).

3. *isixsigma,* s.v. "Six sigma evolution clarified—letter to the editor" (by Daniel T. Lau, January 27, 2002). http://www.isixsigma.com/library/content/c020131a.asp, (accessed January 18, 2006).

Chapter Twenty-Nine: Celebrating Your Cats' Meows

1. *Ethics of the Fathers* is a tractate of the Mishnah, a component of the Talmud. Translation from the original Aramaic by Jeffrey Eisenberg.

2. Holly Buchanan. "Logitech—marketing technology to women," *Marketing to Women Online: How to Shatter Stereotypes and Understand What She Really Wants* (December 11, 2005). http://marketingtowomenonline.typepad.com/blog/2005/12/logitech_market.html, (accessed January 18, 2006).